THE WILD HISTORY OF THE AMERICAN WEST

BLEEDING KANSAS AND THE VIOLENT CLASH OVER SLAVERY IN THE HEARTLAND

Jeff C. Young

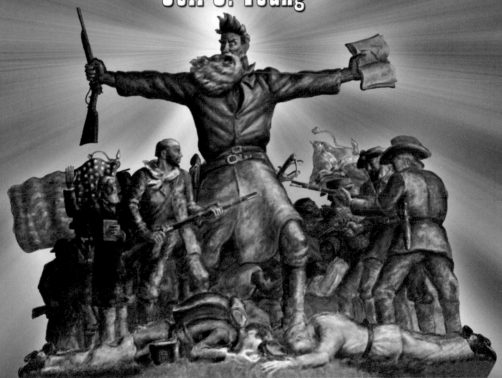

MyReportLinks.com Books

an imprint of

 Enslow Publishers, Inc.

Box 398, 40 Industrial Road
Berkeley Heights, NJ 07922
USA

To my niece, Erin Marie Hundley

MyReportLinks.com Books, an imprint of Enslow Publishers, Inc. MyReportLinks®
is a registered trademark of Enslow Publishers, Inc.

Library of Congress Cataloging-in-Publication Data

Young, Jeff C., 1948–
  Bleeding Kansas and the violent clash over slavery in the heartland / Jeff C. Young.
    p. cm. — (The wild history of the American West)
  Includes bibliographical references and index.
  ISBN 1-59845-013-1
  1. Kansas—History—1854–1861—Juvenile literature. I. Title. II. Series.
  F685.Y68 2006
  978.1'02—dc22

                                2005031013

Printed in the United States of America

10 9 8 7 6 5 4 3 2 1

To Our Readers:
Through the purchase of this book, you and your library gain access to the Report Links that specifically
back up this book.
The Publisher will provide access to the Report Links that back up this book and will keep these Report
Links up to date on **www.myreportlinks.com** for five years from the book's first publication date.
We have done our best to make sure all Internet addresses in this book were active and appropriate when
we went to press. However, the author and the Publisher have no control over, and assume no liability
for, the material available on those Internet sites or on other Web sites they may link to.
The usage of the MyReportLinks.com Books Web site is subject to the terms and conditions stated on the
Usage Policy Statement on **www.myreportlinks.com.**
A password may be required to access the Report Links that back up this book. The password is found
on the bottom of page 4 of this book.
Any comments or suggestions can be sent by e-mail to comments@myreportlinks.com or to the address
on the back cover.

Photo Credits: Photo Credits: Abraham Lincoln Historical Digitization Project, p. 30; Assumption
College, p. 45; B. Davis Schwartz Memorial Library, p. 60; © Corel Corporation, p. 7 (locomotive);
Courtesy of *Dictionary of American Portraits*, © 1967 Dover Publications, Inc., p. 63; CST Washington
University, p. 85; Exploring Constitutional Conflicts, p. 115; Hall Center for the Humanities, p. 40;
Harriet Beecher Stowe House, p. 23; John Simkin, p. 56; Lecompton Historical Society or Kansas State
Historical Society, p. 35; Library of Congress, pp. 3, 7 (dog and man panning for gold, American Indian
chief), 11, 15, 22, 25, 26, 31, 36, 38, 49, 50, 54, 58, 67, 72, 76, 78, 81, 82, 87, 89, 97, 102, 104–105,
110, 112, 114, 116; Kansas Collection, p. 65; Kansas State Historical Society, p. 20; MyReportLinks.com
Books, p. 4; National Archives, p. 12; PBS/WGBH, p. 17; Photography House, p. 1; Photos.com, p. 7 (buf-
falo and wagon train); Sandra Thomas, p. 100; Territorial Kansas Online, p. 42; The Gilder Lehrman
Institute of American History, p. 14; The History Place, p. 29; The KS Gen Web Project, p. 91; The Rector
and Visitors of the University of Virginia, p. 84; The Texas State Historical Association, pp. 75, 77; The
White House, p. 43; United States History/CU in the City, p. 68; University of Kansas, p. 51; University
of Virginia, p. 47; U.S. Department of the Interior, pp. 94, 108, 111; WGBH Educational Foundation, p. 10.

Cover Photo: Photography House

Cover Discription: John Brown is the focus of John Steuart Curry's famous mural "The Tragic Prelude."

CONTENTS

MyReportLinks.com Books
Great Books, Great Links, Great for Research!

The Internet sites featured in this book can save you hours of research time. These Internet sites—we call them **"Report Links"**—are constantly changing, but we keep them up to date on our Web site.

When you see this "Approved Web Site" logo, you will know that we are directing you to a great Internet site that will help you with your research.

Give it a try! Type http://www.myreportlinks.com into your browser, click on the series title and enter the password, then click on the book title, and scroll down to the Report Links listed for this book.

The Report Links will bring you to great source documents, photographs, and illustrations. MyReportLinks.com Books save you time, feature Report Links that are kept up to date, and make report writing easier than ever! A complete listing of the Report Links can be found on pages 118–119 at the back of the book.

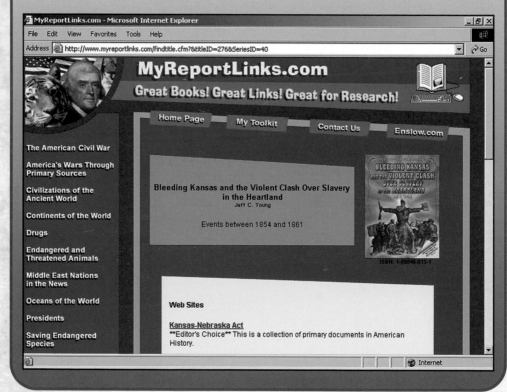

Please see "To Our Readers" on the copyright page for important information about this book, the MyReportLinks.com Web site, and the Report Links that back up this book.

Please enter **WBK1259** if asked for a password.

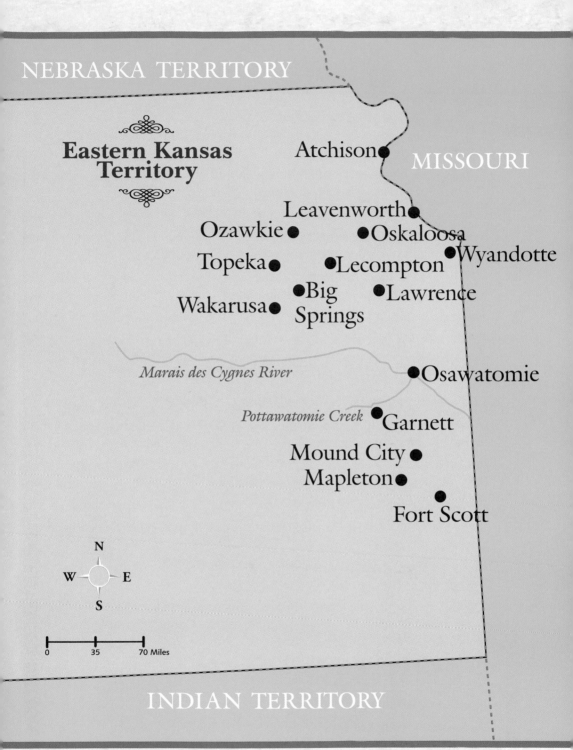

NEBRASKA TERRITORY

Eastern Kansas Territory

Atchison●

MISSOURI

Leavenworth●

Ozawkie●   ●Oskaloosa

Topeka●   ●Lecompton   ●Wyandotte

Wakarusa●   ●Big Springs   ●Lawrence

Marais des Cygnes River

●Osawatomie

Pottawatomie Creek ●Garnett

Mound City●

Mapleton●

●Fort Scott

N
W ● E
S

0   35   70 Miles

INDIAN TERRITORY

▲ This map shows the location of the most important places in the conflict known as Bleeding Kansas.

▷ **1854**—*May 26:* Congress passes the Kansas-Nebraska Act. President Franklin Pierce signs it into law on May 30.

—*July 28:* First organized band of antislavery settlers arrive in Kansas Territory. The town of Lawrence is soon founded by them.

—*October 7:* First territorial governor, Andrew Reeder, arrives in Kansas.

—*November 29:* Governor Reeder oversees first election in Kansas Territory. John W. Whitfield is elected to Congress as the territory's delegate.

▷ **1855**—*March 30:* Election of members to the territorial legislature. An influx of Border Ruffians from Missouri results in a landslide victory for the pro-slavery forces.

—*July 2:* First meeting of the territorial legislature in Pawnee.

—*August 14:* First convention of free-staters meets in Lawrence. They call for the election of delegates to a free-state constitutional convention.

—*August 16:* Reeder is replaced by Wilson Shannon.

—*September 5:* Free-staters meet in Big Springs and form the Free State party.

—*October 23:* Free-staters meet in Topeka and draft their own constitution, which prohibits slavery, and they unofficially "elect" Charles Robinson governor.

—*November 21:* The killing of an antislavery settler by a pro-slavery settler sets off the "Wakarusa War," but there are no casualties.

—*December 15:* Topeka Constitution is approved by the Free State voters.

▷ **1856**—*January 24:* President Pierce declares the Topeka government to be in open rebellion.

—*May 21:* Sheriff Samuel Jones and his pro-slavery posse sack the town of Lawrence.

—*May 22:* Massachusetts Senator Charles Sumner is beaten by South Carolina Congressman Preston Brooks after Sumner's "The Crime Against Kansas" speech.

—*May 24:* Five pro-slavery settlers are killed by John Brown and his cohorts in the Pottawatomie Massacre.

—*June 30:* Congress rejects the Topeka Constitution.

—*August 18:* Governor Shannon removed from office.

—*August 30:* Five killed in the Battle of Osawatomie.

—*September 9:* John W. Geary becomes governor.

—*October 6:* Election of territorial legislature. Election is largely boycotted by free-state men.

—*November 4:* James Buchanan elected president.

—*November 29:* J. W. Whitfield elected territorial delegate to Congress.

▷ **1857** —*January 7:* Free-state legislature meets in Topeka.

—*March 20:* Governor Geary resigns.

—*March 24:* New governor Robert J. Walker arrives in Kansas.

—*July 14:* Governor Walker declares Lawrence is in open rebellion for establishing an illegal government.

—*September 7:* Constitutional Convention meets in Lecompton.

—*October 5–6:* Free-staters elect a majority to the territorial legislature.

—*December 17:* Governor Walker resigns.

—*December 21:* James W. Denver becomes acting governor. Pro-slavery Lecompton Constitution is approved in a statewide election boycotted by Free-state voters.

▷ **1858** —*January 4:* Lecompton Constitution is rejected in a second election.

—*May 18:* Leavenworth Constitution is approved by Kansas voters but rejected by Congress.

—*May 19:* Eleven people killed in the Marais des Cygnes Massacre.

—*August 2:* In a third and final vote, Kansans reject the Lecompton Constitution.

▷ **1859** —*July 5:* A fourth constitutional convention convenes in Wyandotte.

—*October 4:* Kansas voters approve the antislavery Wyandotte Constitution by a vote of 10,420 to 5,530.

— *December 6:* Charles Robinson elected governor under the Wyandotte Constitution.

▷ **1860** —*April 11:* Wyandotte Constitution approved by the U.S. House of Representatives.

—*November 6:* Abraham Lincoln elected president.

▷ **1861** —*January 21:* U.S. Senate approves the Wyandotte Constitution.

—*January 29:* Before leaving office, President Buchanan signs bill admitting Kansas to the Union as a free state.

Chapter 1 ▶

JOHN BROWN AND THE POTTAWATOMIE MASSACRE

John Brown was an angry and dangerous man. He hated slavery, and he was willing to kill people who supported it. Back in 1837, at a church service in Ohio, Brown had stood up and announced to the congregation, "Here before God in the presence of these witnesses, I consecrate my life to the destruction of slavery."[1] While living in Pennsylvania, Brown became an agent for the Underground Railroad. He had lived in an African-American community in New York, and helped free blacks in Massachusetts and protected fugitive slaves.[2]

In 1855, five of Brown's sons were among the thousands of settlers moving into the Kansas Territory. An election would be held to determine if Kansas would enter the Union as a free state or as a slave-holding state. Pro-slavery and antislavery forces were fighting to seize political control.

Sometime in the spring of 1855, Brown received an alarming letter from John, Jr., his son. Brown's son wrote that thousands of pro-slavery settlers were migrating to Kansas. They wanted to ensure the expansion of slavery into the territory.

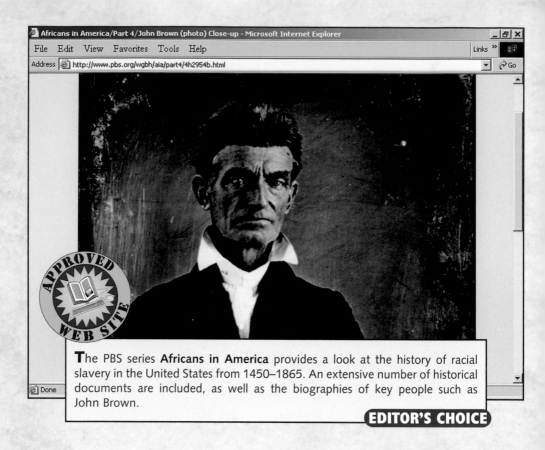

Africans in America/Part 4/John Brown (photo) Close-up - Microsoft Internet Explorer

File   Edit   View   Favorites   Tools   Help   Links »

Address http://www.pbs.org/wgbh/aia/part4/4h2954b.html   Go

The PBS series **Africans in America** provides a look at the history of racial slavery in the United States from 1450–1865. An extensive number of historical documents are included, as well as the biographies of key people such as John Brown.

EDITOR'S CHOICE

John, Jr., wrote that they were "armed to the teeth with Revolvers, Bowie Knives and Cannon."[3]

The next day, Brown decided to leave his farm in North Elba, New York, to go to Kansas. After selling his cattle to finance the journey, Brown packed a wagon and headed west. "I'm going to Kansas to make it a free state," Brown declared.[4]

▶ **Fund-Raising**

Along with the alarming news of an armed invasion of Border Ruffians, John, Jr.'s, letter included a plea for more weapons. He wrote that the antislavery forces badly needed arms. "Now we want for you to get for us these arms. We need them more than we do bread."[5]

Before heading west, Brown contacted other abolitionists (people who wanted to end slavery) and asked them for money to aid their cause. Along the way, Brown also stopped at Syracuse, New York, to attend a convention of abolitionists. At the convention, Brown made an emotional speech pleading for money to bring arms to the antislavery settlers in the Kansas Territory.

Brown only raised about sixty dollars, but he was not discouraged. In his life, he had suffered many setbacks. Brown had a long history of failure in various enterprises. Along with farming, he had worked as a surveyor, a leather tanner, and a real estate speculator. But in abolitionism, he found something pure and noble to give his life meaning and purpose.

During a stop in Akron, Ohio, Brown

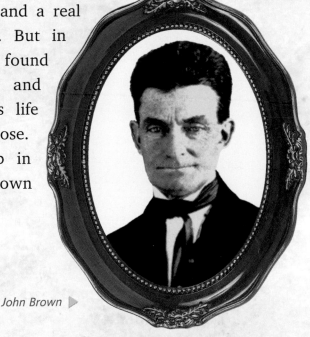

John Brown ▶

▲ *John Steuart Curry illustrated this famous mural of John Brown called "The Tragic Prelude." The mural is at the statehouse in Topeka, Kansas.*

was more successful in getting support for his cause. At a meeting in a public hall, he was able to collect some ammunition and clothing. He also acquired about ten broadswords that would later be used in Kansas.

On August 18, Brown left Cleveland, Ohio, with his son-in-law, Henry Thompson. Then, they traveled to Detroit and picked up his sixteen-year-old son, Oliver. The trio arrived at the Osawatomie settlement in Kansas on October 7. Brown only had sixty cents left when he arrived, but all of the weapons were still intact. He established a small fort that he called Brown's Station and recruited other antislavery settlers to form a militia called the Pottawatomie Rifles.

Violence in Kansas

When Brown arrived, there had already been several skirmishes between the pro-slavery and antislavery forces. During the next six months, things would get worse.

Brown and the members of his militia would keep a watchful eye on the pro-slavery settlers who were moving into the area of Kansas alongside Pottawatomie Creek.

Despite their activities, the men of the Pottawatomie Rifles were unable to foresee or prevent a band of pro-slavery settlers from Missouri from attacking an antislavery settlement in Lawrence, Kansas, in May 1856. After learning that none of the abolitionists had fired a single shot in self-defense during what came to be known as the Sack of Lawrence, Brown decided to avenge the attack. On May 23, he convened some militia

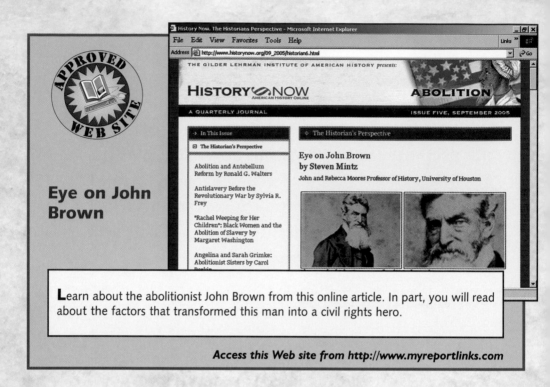

Eye on John Brown

THE GILDER LEHRMAN INSTITUTE OF AMERICAN HISTORY *presents:*

HISTORY NOW
AMERICAN HISTORY ONLINE

ABOLITION

A QUARTERLY JOURNAL

ISSUE FIVE, SEPTEMBER 2005

→ In This Issue

☐ The Historian's Perspective

Abolition and Antebellum Reform by Ronald G. Walters

Antislavery Before the Revolutionary War by Sylvia R. Frey

"Rachel Weeping for Her Children": Black Women and the Abolition of Slavery by Margaret Washington

Angelina and Sarah Grimke: Abolitionist Sisters by Carol Berkin

◆ The Historian's Perspective

Eye on John Brown
by Steven Mintz
John and Rebecca Moores Professor of History, University of Houston

Learn about the abolitionist John Brown from this online article. In part, you will read about the factors that transformed this man into a civil rights hero.

Access this Web site from http://www.myreportlinks.com

members for a secret operation. The next day, the operation was underway.

▷ Massacre at Pottawatomie Creek

Under the cover of darkness, Brown and his men moved along the banks of Pottawatomie Creek. They quietly closed in on the cabin of James Doyle. Doyle was a pro-slavery settler who had moved to Kansas from Tennessee.

When he heard a knock on his door, Doyle cautiously asked who was there. Brown told Doyle that they were looking for the cabin of another pro-slavery settler named Allen Wilkinson. Doyle then made the fatal mistake of opening his door.

That allowed Brown and his well-armed men to storm the cabin. Brown told the terror-stricken Doyle that the Northern army had come to see him. Brown ordered Doyle and his three sons to leave the cabin.

Doyle's frightened wife begged and pleaded with Brown to let their fourteen-year-old son stay inside. Brown mercifully let him stay. Then, Doyle and his two older sons, William and Drury, were escorted outside.

▲ This lithograph by Joseph Hoover was called "Heroes of the Colored Race."
The three large portraits in the middle are of Blanche Kelso Bruce, Frederick Douglass, and Hiram Rhoades Revels. John Brown is included in the mural. He is in the middle of the bottom row.

Brown quietly stood back and watched his two sons, Salmon and Owen, viciously kill the three unarmed men. Before trying to flee, the Doyles bravely and gamely tried to defend themselves. Both fight and flight were futile efforts against two sword-swinging attackers. In a matter of minutes, the Doyles were hacked to death. Their arms were severed and their heads were split open. Then, Brown drew his pistol and fired a single shot into James Doyle's forehead.

Brown was not ready to end the killing spree. He led his men a half mile away from the Doyle's cabin to the Wilkinson cabin. Allen Wilkinson became their fourth victim. He pleaded for mercy because his wife was sick with the measles and needed a caretaker. His pleas were ignored. Two of Brown's sons hacked Wilkinson to death with their broadswords.

On their final stop, Brown and his cohorts made a pro-slavery settler named William Sherman their fifth victim. Sherman was seized from the cabin of his friend, James Harris, and led away to the Pottawatomie Creek. On the creek bank, Sherman was beheaded.

The murderers were also thieves. They stole horses, saddles, and a bowie knife from their victims. In Brown's mind, he and his cohorts had done nothing wrong. They were merely punishing evil men for supporting the sinful practice of slavery.

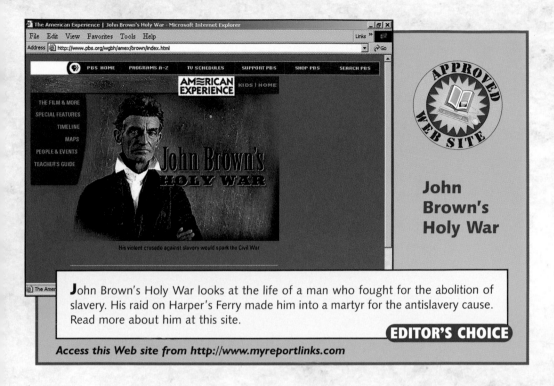

The American Experience | John Brown's Holy War - Microsoft Internet Explorer

File   Edit   View   Favorites   Tools   Help   Links »

Address   http://www.pbs.org/wgbh/amex/brown/index.html

PBS HOME   PROGRAMS A-Z   TV SCHEDULES   SUPPORT PBS   SHOP PBS   SEARCH PBS

AMERICAN EXPERIENCE   KIDS | HOME

THE FILM & MORE
SPECIAL FEATURES
TIMELINE
MAPS
PEOPLE & EVENTS
TEACHER'S GUIDE

John Brown's
HOLY WAR

His violent crusade against slavery would spark the Civil War

John Brown's Holy War

John Brown's Holy War looks at the life of a man who fought for the abolition of slavery. His raid on Harper's Ferry made him into a martyr for the antislavery cause. Read more about him at this site.

EDITOR'S CHOICE

Access this Web site from http://www.myreportlinks.com

▶ Eruption of Violence

The news of John Brown's "Pottawatomie Massacre" ended whatever uneasy peace there still was between the pro-slavery Border Ruffians and the antislavery free-state faction. The news spread quickly, but it was not reported accurately. Different sides offered different stories. One version blamed the attack on American Indians. Another version claimed that the killings never occurred.

When territorial governor Wilson Shannon heard about the massacre, he feared that the territory would erupt in an all-out civil war. He dispatched troops to Osawatomie and Lawrence. He wrote to President Franklin Pierce saying that the murders had "produced an extraordinary state of excitement" and added, "I hope that the offenders may be brought to justice, otherwise, I fear the consequences."[6]

Governor Shannon's fears would be realized. In the southeastern sector of Kansas, chaos reigned. Both pro-slavery and free-state settlers fled for their lives. Armed bands of men prowled the area shooting one another and looting stores and homes.

This would not be the last of the random acts of violence to occur in the territory that came to be known as Bleeding Kansas.

FREE STATES VERSUS SLAVE STATES

When the United States completed the Louisiana Purchase in 1803, the young nation acquired over 800,000 square miles of land for $15 million. America's western border moved from the Mississippi River to the Rocky Mountains.

In the early 1800s, there was a basic understanding among lawmakers that slavery would be legal in the southern states, illegal in the northern states, and would not be allowed to spread into the newly acquired territories. As pioneers moved westward to settle in the newly acquired territories, a persistent problem arose. How could the growing nation expand its borders without limiting the practice of slavery? In fact, at the time that the U.S. Constitution was written the founding fathers had banned the spread of slavery in the Northwest Territories.[1] At the time, that was the only part of the United States that had not been carved into states. That understanding looked like it might come to an end when Missouri applied for statehood in 1819.

http://www.kshs.org/cool3/graphics/ginlg.jpg - Microsoft Internet Explorer

File   Edit   View   Favorites   Tools   Help   Links »

Address http://www.kshs.org/cool3/graphics/ginlg.jpg   Go

Done

The invention of the cotton gin allowed plantation owners to produce large amounts of cotton. As a result, they sought out open land and needed more slaves to work the large fields. The **Topics in Kansas History: Settlement (1830–1890)** Web site from the Kansas State Historical Society provides a brief, but detailed history of the settlement of Kansas.

EDITOR'S CHOICE

▶ Missouri Compromise

At that time, there were twenty-two states in the Union. Eleven of them were slave states, and the other eleven were free states. Adding Missouri as a free state or as a slave state would upset that perfect balance of power. This is because the addition of another state would mean that either the slave states or the free states would have more votes in Congress. This was especially important in the Senate where there are only two Senators per state.

After a long and bitter debate, Congress passed a law known as the Missouri Compromise. The compromise maintained the balance of power by allowing Missouri to join the Union as a slave state, while permitting Maine to be admitted as a free state. The compromise also outlawed slavery in any territory north of latitude 36 degrees 30 minutes (36°30′).

The Missouri Compromise was able to establish an uneasy peace, but neither side was really happy with the law. Antislavery northerners wanted to completely stop the spread of slavery. Pro-slavery southerners did not like the federal government drawing a line that determined where slavery could not exist. They believed that the residents of the individual states or territories should decide if they wanted to allow slavery. The idea of allowing people to vote to decide whether or not to allow slavery in a territory was called popular sovereignty.

Compromise of 1850

Tensions between North and South escalated after the United States acquired additional territory as a result of the Mexican-American War, which lasted from 1846 to 1848. By defeating Mexico, the United States acquired an additional 525,000 square miles of territory. Soon, Congress was debating whether slavery would be allowed in

▲ The title of this painting was "Union," by Tompkins H. Matteson. The illustration was created soon after the Compromise of 1850, when people were hopeful that the compromise would ease the nation's arguments over slavery.

these newly acquired territories. Once again, the same opposing forces put forth the same arguments. Northerners opposed any expansion of slavery and southerners felt the residents of the new territories should decide. A new compromise solution was agreed upon.

Three powerful and respected senators—Stephen Douglas of Illinois, Henry Clay of Kentucky, and Daniel Webster of Massachusetts—ironed out a solution known as the Compromise of 1850. Under this compromise, California would join the Union as a free state, but the issue of slavery in the Utah and New Mexico territories would be decided by the people living there. The new compromise delayed a civil war between the North and South, but once again, both sides were still unsatisfied.

Northerners were offended by a provision in the compromise known as the Fugitive Slave Law. The Fugitive Slave Law made it easier for slaveholders to recover slaves who had run away and

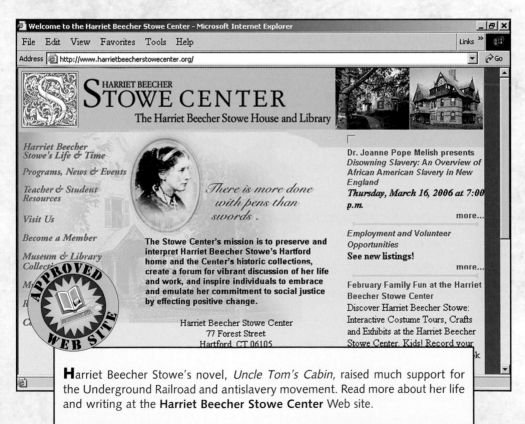

Harriet Beecher Stowe's novel, *Uncle Tom's Cabin,* raised much support for the Underground Railroad and antislavery movement. Read more about her life and writing at the **Harriet Beecher Stowe Center** Web site.

sought freedom by escaping to free states. Anyone identified and captured as a runaway slave could be returned to his or her owner without any kind of trial by jury. Antislavery Northerners living in free states could also be forced to aid in the capture of suspected runaway slaves.

Southerners were dissatisfied with the new compromise because the admission of California as a free state shifted the balance of power in Congress. California's 1850 admission as the thirty-first state changed the totals to fifteen slave states and sixteen free states.

Uncle Tom's Cabin

In 1851 and 1852, an antislavery newspaper, the *National Era,* published a series of fictional stories about a Kentucky slave named Uncle Tom. In 1852, the stories by Harriet Beecher Stowe were published as a book entitled *Uncle Tom's Cabin.*

The book depicted the horrific practices of slavery—whippings and beatings by cruel slave masters, the hard forced labor without pay, and the breakup of families when slaves were sold off to different owners. *Uncle Tom's Cabin* got many Americans to start regarding slavery as a moral issue instead of a legal one. It became an immediate best seller. In less than a year, Beecher Stowe's work sold around three hundred thousand copies.

▲ *Harriet Beecher Stowe, author of* Uncle Tom's Cabin.

Kansas-Nebraska Act

As tensions between Northerners and Southerners mounted, settlers began moving into the territories of Kansas and Nebraska. Thousands of small farmers, merchants, and tradesmen migrated to the new territories. Most of them were unconcerned about whether slavery would be extended or ended. They merely wanted to better themselves economically.

Since the growing populations of the Kansas and Nebraska territories would be seeking to join the Union, Congress would have to decide if slavery would be allowed or abolished there.

American Memory Digital Item Display - 2004663930 - Microsoft Internet Explorer

File   Edit   View   Favorites   Tools   Help   Links »

Address http://memory.loc.gov/cgi-bin/query/I?dag:33:./temp/~ammem_9ZX4::displayType=1:m856sd=cph:m856sf=3c10141:@@@mdb=mcc,g   Go

Done

Stephen Douglas was the author of the Kansas-Nebraska Act. The Library of Congress site, **The "Show Me" State** links to information about Douglas and how his act affected the pro-slavery citizens of Missouri.

Stephen Douglas offered a bill to settle the issue. Douglas hoped that his bill, known as the Kansas-Nebraska Act, would be acceptable to both the North and the South.

Stephen Douglas was a senator from Illinois. He did not have any strong feelings about slavery. His main concern was for the vast Midwestern territories between the Rocky Mountains and the Missouri River to be settled so a transcontinental railroad could be built. A transcontinental railroad would help settle the Great Plains region. Douglas wanted the railroad to run through Chicago, so that Illinois businesses would profit by selling goods to the settlers in the Great Plains and beyond. That would produce great economic benefits for Illinois and possibly advance his political career.[2]

New Territories

The bill would create two separate territories: the Kansas Territory and the Nebraska Territory, which would eventually become states. Douglas's original bill did not address the issue of slavery in the new territory. The Nebraska Territory was north of the 36°30′ line established by the Missouri Compromise. Presumably, that settled the issue of slavery in the Nebraska Territory. Slavery had no legal right to exist there.

Southern senators found that totally unacceptable. They demanded that Douglas add a clause to permit slavery and repeal the line established by the Missouri Compromise. Bowing to their demands, Douglas added a provision that said the slavery issue would be decided by a vote of the people living in the Nebraska Territory. This was known as popular sovereignty.

That was not enough to satisfy the southerners. Douglas further amended his bill to please them. The final bill specifically repealed the Missouri Compromise and created two territories—Kansas and Nebraska—instead of just one. The prevailing political opinion was that the settlers of Nebraska would not vote to allow slavery, but Kansas might. Douglas argued that the climate of Nebraska would not warrant the type of large-scale farming that might need slaves to operate. "He believed conditions of climate and soil would effectively keep slavery out of Kansas and Nebraska. But the fact remained that his bill threw land open to slavery where it had been prohibited before."[3]

▶ Differing Opinion

Abraham Lincoln, then a state legislator from Illinois, gave a speech rejecting Douglas's argument that the climate of the territories did not allow for slavery. Lincoln said:

> As to climate, a glance at the map shows that there are five slave States—Delaware, Maryland, Virginia, Kentucky, and Missouri, and also the

In 1854, Abraham Lincoln was an Illinois legislator that questioned the Kansas-Nebraska Act. The **Abraham Lincoln** Web site contains a complete biography of his life.

District of Columbia, all north of the Missouri Compromise line. The census returns of 1850 show that within these there are eight hundred and sixty-seven thousand two hundred and seventy-six slaves, being more than one fourth of all the slaves in the nation.[4]

Although many Northern Democrats opposed Douglas's amended bill, President Franklin Pierce endorsed the measure. Even with presidential support, Douglas's bill was held up by a lengthy congressional debate. On May 22, 1854, the House of Representatives passed Douglas's bill by a vote of 113 to 100. Three days later, the Senate approved the measure by a thirty-five to thirteen vote. President Pierce signed the bill into law on May 30, 1854.

The vote was divided along geographical lines. Almost all the Southern members of Congress voted for it. About half of the Northern Democrats in the House voted against it; several other Democrats wanted to, but loyalty to their party kept them in line.

Douglas knew that the passage of the Kansas-Nebraska Act would intensify the debate over slavery. Yet, he believed that popular sovereignty would be the solution to satisfy everyone. He was sadly mistaken.

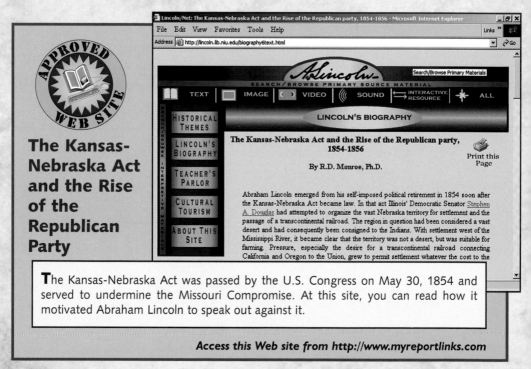

The Kansas-Nebraska Act and the Rise of the Republican Party

The Kansas-Nebraska Act was passed by the U.S. Congress on May 30, 1854 and served to undermine the Missouri Compromise. At this site, you can read how it motivated Abraham Lincoln to speak out against it.

Access this Web site from http://www.myreportlinks.com

▲ Franklin Pierce was the fourteenth president of the United States. He was elected in 1852.

The Kansas-Nebraska Act has been called the law that ripped America in two. It forever altered the political structure of the country. The gulf between antislavery Northern Democrats and the pro-slavery Southern Democrats grew so wide that the Northerners left to join the emerging Republican party. The Northern and Southern Whigs were similarly divided over the slavery issue. Ultimately, the Democratic party was torn apart. The Whig party ceased to be a major political force in America, and the Republican party was created.

Emergence of the Republican Party

Shortly after the passage of the Kansas-Nebraska Act, "Anti-Nebraska" protest meetings were held throughout America. Two of those meetings occurred in Ripon, Wisconsin, on February 28 and March 20, 1854. A coalition of abolitionists, Whigs, and Democrats attended. They decided to call themselves Republicans because they believed they were the political descendants of Thomas Jefferson's Democratic-Republican Party.

On July 6, 1854, the Republicans held their first statewide convention in Jackson, Michigan, and formally adopted the name Republicans. The new party experienced a rapid growth. In the 1854 midterm congressional elections, the Republicans became the majority party in the House of

Representatives by winning 108 seats. In addition, they won fifteen seats in the U.S. Senate.

As a new antislavery party emerged, battle lines were drawn in Kansas between the pro-slavery "Border Ruffians" from Missouri and the antislavery settlers.

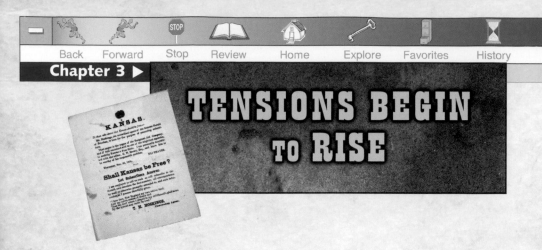

Chapter 3

TENSIONS BEGIN TO RISE

When President Franklin Pierce appointed the first territorial governor of Kansas, he chose a loyal Democrat who would help to strengthen the Democratic party there. His choice was Andrew H. Reeder, an undistinguished Pennsylvania lawyer who had never held political office. Although he was appointed on June 29, 1854, Reeder waited until autumn to settle in Kansas.

Reeder's first official action as governor was to order the election of a territorial delegate to Congress. Reeder vainly hoped for an honest election, and he issued a proclamation defining exactly what a residence in Kansas was. The proclamation said the voter could only have one residence, which had to be in the Kansas Territory. Furthermore, the voter had to intend to make that residence his permanent home.

▶ Voter Fraud

The election was held on November 29, 1854. Reeder's proclamation was ignored, and there was widespread fraud. Missourians came into Kansas

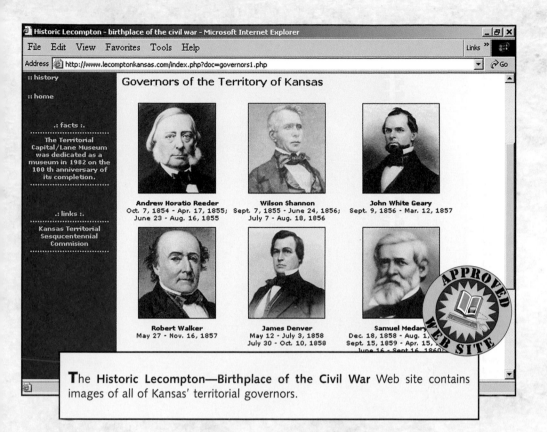

Historic Lecompton - birthplace of the civil war - Microsoft Internet Explorer

File Edit View Favorites Tools Help   Links »

Address http://www.lecomptonkansas.com/index.php?doc=governors1.php   Go

:: history
:: home

.: facts :.
The Territorial
Capital/Lane Museum
was dedicated as a
museum in 1982 on the
100 th anniversary of
its completion.

.: links :.
Kansas Territorial
Sesquecentennial
Commision

Governors of the Territory of Kansas

Andrew Horatio Reeder
Oct. 7, 1854 - Apr. 17, 1855;
June 23 - Aug. 16, 1855

Wilson Shannon
Sept. 7, 1855 - June 24, 1856;
July 7 - Aug. 18, 1856

John White Geary
Sept. 9, 1856 - Mar. 12, 1857

Robert Walker
May 27 - Nov. 16, 1857

James Denver
May 12 - July 3, 1858
July 30 - Oct. 10, 1858

Samuel Medary
Dec. 18, 1858 - Aug. 1,
Sept. 15, 1859 - Apr. 15,
June 16 - Sept. 16, 1860

The **Historic Lecompton—Birthplace of the Civil War** Web site contains images of all of Kansas' territorial governors.

in large numbers and voted for the pro-slavery candidate, J. W. Whitfield. Antislavery voters felt overwhelmed and intimidated by the force of numbers. Most antislavery residents did not even vote.

In early December 1854, it was announced that J. W. Whitfield was elected as the congressional delegate with 2,258 votes. A later congressional investigation would conclude that there were more than seventeen hundred fraudulent votes in that election. In one precinct known as 110, 584 of the 604 votes cast were later determined to be fraudulent.

▲ Henry Ward Beecher was an abolitionist preacher from Connecticut. He raised money to supply weapons to antislavery settlers in Kansas. These weapons came to be known as Beecher's Bibles.

Governor Reeder had the authority to challenge the results, but he chose to let them stand. Even without the widespread fraud and intimidation, the pro-slavery side would have won. They simply had more people in Kansas at that time.

Governor Reeder had set March 30, 1855, as the date for electing a territorial legislature. The pro-slavery side was concerned that they could lose that election. They feared that a large migration of antislavery voters into Kansas would decide the outcome.

▶ Organizations on Both Sides

Their fears were well founded. Eli Thayer, a member of the Massachusetts legislature, had founded the New England Emigrant Aid Company (NEEAC). Its purpose was to encourage antislavery northerners to settle in the Kansas and Nebraska territories. By 1855, the NEEAC had brought about two thousand antislavery settlers into Kansas. They founded several communities in Kansas. "The abolitionists pumped in, armed with "Beecher's Bibles" (rifles) and the printing press, an equally important weapon, to keep the state free."[1]

Supporting the pro-slavery forces there were organizations known as Blue Lodges or Self-Defensives. They were secretive societies dedicated to extending slavery into Kansas. They enticed

▲ Eli Thayer was an abolitionist from Massachusetts. He was also a lawmaker and a judge.

Missourians to vote in Kansas by offering them "free ferry (transportation), a dollar a day & liquor."[2]

David Atchison

Missouri Senator David Rice Atchison was the most prominent politician to support the pro-slavery Border Ruffians. In January 1855, he rallied the pro-slavery forces by writing

> The Abolitionists will make great efforts in the spring to send into Kansas their battalions & Regts. for the holy purpose of excluding Slaveholders. They should be met by corresponding efforts on our part. We can and must defeat them and nothing that is fair and honorable should be left undone.[3]

As election day neared, Atchison and his supporters stepped up their efforts to recruit voters, raise money, and strategize. Three days prior to the election, ferries were carrying eight hundred voters a day across the Missouri River into Kansas. At Leavenworth, Kansas, the number of recorded votes was five times the number of registered voters. According to the territorial census, there were 2,905 registered voters in Kansas, but over 6,000 men voted in March 30 election. There was a total of 5,427 pro-slavery votes. Atchison's planning and preparation paid off, but the voter fraud was so flagrant and widespread, many people thought that he and his cohorts went too far.

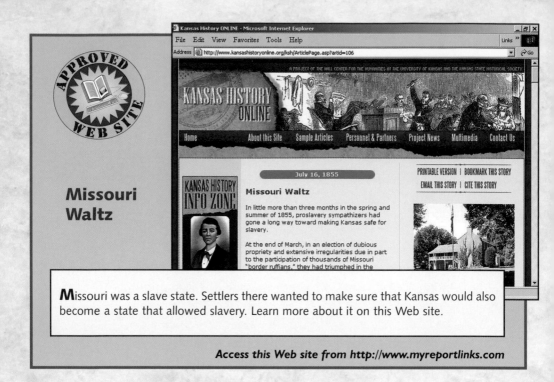

Missouri Waltz

Kansas History ONLINE - Microsoft Internet Explorer

File   Edit   View   Favorites   Tools   Help   Links

Address http://www.kansashistoryonline.org/ksh/ArticlePage.asp?artid=106   Go

A PROJECT OF THE HALL CENTER FOR THE HUMANITIES AT THE UNIVERSITY OF KANSAS AND THE KANSAS STATE HISTORICAL SOCIETY

KANSAS HISTORY ONLINE

Home   About this Site   Sample Articles   Personnel & Partners   Project News   Multimedia   Contact Us

July 16, 1855

PRINTABLE VERSION | BOOKMARK THIS STORY
EMAIL THIS STORY | CITE THIS STORY

Missouri Waltz

In little more than three months in the spring and summer of 1855, proslavery sympathizers had gone a long way toward making Kansas safe for slavery.

At the end of March, in an election of dubious propriety and extensive irregularities due in part to the participation of thousands of Missouri "border ruffians," they had triumphed in the

Missouri was a slave state. Settlers there wanted to make sure that Kansas would also become a state that allowed slavery. Learn more about it on this Web site.

Access this Web site from http://www.myreportlinks.com

There were a few muted protests from antislavery voters. A Missouri newspaper, the *Parkville Luminary,* ran a story objecting to the widespread lawlessness and voter fraud in Kansas. A mob of two hundred people threw their printing press into the Missouri River and ordered the editor and publisher to leave the state.

William Phillips, an antislavery lawyer from Leavenworth, filed a formal protest about election and voter irregularities in his district. A committee of a dozen men took Phillips into their custody. They shaved half of his head, tarred and feathered him, and rode him on a rail for a mile and a half, which meant that he was on public display in this humiliating state.

On April 6, Governor Reeder voided the results in six disputed legislative districts. He ordered a special election to be held on May 22. The election was mostly peaceful, but the results were the same. About three fourths of the newly elected legislators were pro-slavery.

After the second election, Reeder went to Washington, D.C., and met with President Pierce, because Reeder still suspected fraud. He asked Pierce to approve a new election and send military forces to Kansas to ensure fair results. Although he was a New Englander, President Pierce was not opposed to slavery. He believed that it had a legal right to exist and even expand into new territories if popular sovereignty supported it. Reeder claimed that Pierce supported him, but a new election was not held. Reeder returned to Kansas to face a hostile legislature. Fearing further violence, Reeder decided to let the election results stand.

Pro-Slavery Legislature

In protest of the election results, many of the anti-slavery legislators resigned their seats. They did not want any part of a government that had seized power through fraud and intimidation. The ones who did not resign found themselves expelled

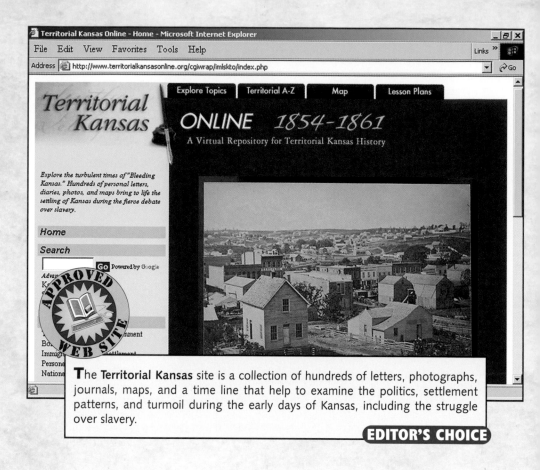

Territorial Kansas Online - Home - Microsoft Internet Explorer

File   Edit   View   Favorites   Tools   Help   Links »

Address http://www.territorialkansasonline.org/cgiwrap/imlskto/index.php   Go

Explore Topics   Territorial A-Z   Map   Lesson Plans

Territorial Kansas

ONLINE   *1854-1861*

A Virtual Repository for Territorial Kansas History

Explore the turbulent times of "Bleeding Kansas." Hundreds of personal letters, diaries, photos, and maps bring to life the settling of Kansas during the fierce debate over slavery.

Home

Search

[Go] Powered by Google

The **Territorial Kansas** site is a collection of hundreds of letters, photographs, journals, maps, and a time line that help to examine the politics, settlement patterns, and turmoil during the early days of Kansas, including the struggle over slavery.

EDITOR'S CHOICE

when the pro-slavery legislature met in Pawnee in July 1855.

Along with expelling the antislavery lawmakers, the pro-slavery legislature enacted a series of pro-slavery laws. Anyone who circulated or wrote antislavery material could be sentenced to two years of hard labor. Stealing slaves, helping to steal slaves, and/or causing slaves to revolt against their owners were punishable by imprisonment or death.

▶ Ousting of Governor Reeder

Shortly after the new legislature convened, Governor Reeder was fighting to hold on to his office. There were charges that he was using his office for personal gain in land speculation. When he chose Pawnee as the territorial capital, Reeder forced the legislature to meet on land that he had invested money in. If Pawnee became the permanent capital, the value of the land would increase.

The legislature rebelled by voting to meet in Shawnee Mission. Reeder vetoed their move. Then, the legislature overrode his veto. Reeder responded by vetoing all the bills the legislature passed. He claimed that since they left Pawnee, the legislature was not meeting legally.

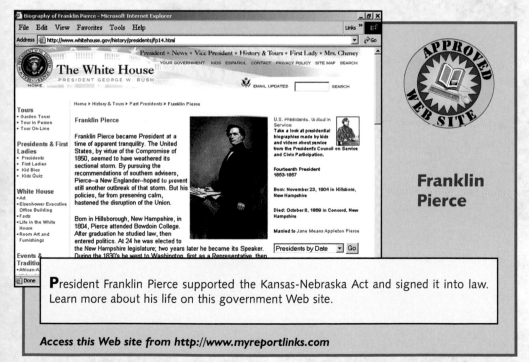

Franklin Pierce

President Franklin Pierce supported the Kansas-Nebraska Act and signed it into law. Learn more about his life on this government Web site.

Access this Web site from http://www.myreportlinks.com

The fight ended after the legislature petitioned President Pierce to remove Reeder from office. On August 15, Reeder received a dismissal notice for his unethical conduct. The official reason give for his dismissal was his land speculations, but the more likely reason was his opposition to the pro-slavery legislature.

Big Springs

Reeder was replaced by Wilson Shannon, a former governor of Ohio. Shannon claimed to be neutral on the issue of slavery, but as a congressman he had supported the Kansas-Nebraska Act. The appoint-ment of Shannon and the enactment of pro-slavery laws moved the antislavery forces to hold a conven-tion at Big Springs in September 1855.

At the convention, the three hundred or so delegates passed a resolution declaring that the current legislature had no legal authority. Their resolution boldly declared in part,

> That we owe no allegiance or obedience to the tyrannical enactments of this spurious Legislature— that their laws have no validity or binding force upon the people of Kansas . . . That we will resist them primarily by every peaceable and legal means within our power, until we can elect our own Representatives. . . . That . . . As soon as we ascer-tain that peaceable remedies shall fail . . . we will endure and submit to these laws no longer . . . and we will resist them to a bloody issue. . . .[4]

The convention at Big Springs organized the antislavery faction into a political party called the Free State party. It was not an abolitionist party, and it believed that slavery could continue to exist in the slave states. The party opposed nonresidents voting in Kansas elections and believed that slavery should not exist in Kansas.

Two Governments

In October 1855, a combination of pro-slavery residents and Border Ruffians from Missouri reelected J. W. Whitfield as the territory's congressional delegate. The members of the Free State party boycotted the election and held their own election. They elected ex-governor Reeder as

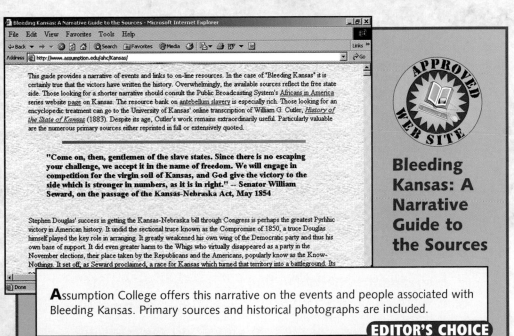

Bleeding Kansas: A Narrative Guide to the Sources

Assumption College offers this narrative on the events and people associated with Bleeding Kansas. Primary sources and historical photographs are included.

EDITOR'S CHOICE

Access this Web site from http://www.myreportlinks.com

the congressional delegate. Reeder contested Whitfield's election, but the Pierce administration recognized Whitfield as the duly elected delegate.

In October and November 1855, the free-staters held their own constitutional convention in Topeka. They drafted a constitution that prohibited slavery in Kansas. Yet, their new constitution also prohibited free blacks from settling in Kansas. They set December 15 as a date for a statewide election to ratify the new constitution.

Wakarusa War

Before the ratification election was held, there was a major confrontation between the pro-slavery and antislavery factions known as the Wakarusa War. This conflict got its name from the nearby Wakarusa River. The confrontation was set off when Charles W. Dow, an antislavery supporter, was shot and killed by Franklin N. Coleman, a pro-slavery leader, on November 21. The two men had been squabbling over some disputed land in or around Hickory Point. Coleman had been squatting on some land claimed by Jacob Branson, who was a friend and roommate of Dow's.

Accounts of the incident give the impression that Dow was unarmed. Coleman claimed that Dow threatened him with a two-foot piece of iron and that he acted in self-defense. Hickory Point was an antislavery settlement. Coleman feared that he could not get a fair trial there, so he took his family and fled to Missouri.

On November 26, Branson held a meeting at his house in Hickory Point. Most of the people there were members of a local militia company. They decided to take the law into their own hands. They appointed a committee to punish Coleman and anyone else who they believed was connected to Dow's murder.

Before the meeting, some antislavery men had already committed some vengeful acts. Armed men had burned down the homes of two pro-slavery men. After the meeting, the violence

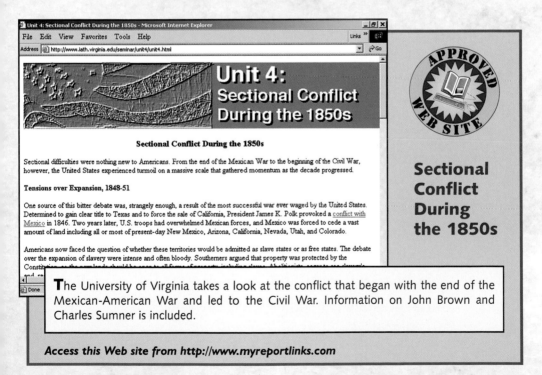

The University of Virginia takes a look at the conflict that began with the end of the Mexican-American War and led to the Civil War. Information on John Brown and Charles Sumner is included.

Access this Web site from http://www.myreportlinks.com

continued. Coleman's abandoned house was burned and destroyed. A few hours later, Branson was arrested by Sheriff Samuel J. Jones.

Branson was in the custody of Jones and his posse when they were surrounded by a group of well-armed antislavery men. The sheriff and his posse were forced to back down and release Branson. Branson's rescuers then escorted him into the antislavery stronghold of Lawrence.

▶ Governor Gets Involved

Sheriff Jones immediately notified Governor Shannon that a group of armed antislavery vigilantes had taken the prisoner from his custody. Shannon then called out the territorial militia. Colonel Edwin Sumner, the local army commander, was unresponsive, so Shannon then called on the people of the territory to help Sheriff Jones subdue what he called "an armed band" of lawless men.[5]

Shannon got much more help than he expected. Pro-slavery Border Ruffians from Missouri flooded into Kansas. It is estimated that in three days somewhere between one thousand to fifteen hundred Missourians answered the call. One observer described the Border Ruffians as "all armed & determined to burn Lawrence."[6]

While the pro-slavers set up camp on the Wakarusa River outside of Lawrence, the antislavery

▲ Colonel Edwin Sumner is shown here after his promotion to
major general during the Civil War.

LIBERTY. THE FAIR MAID OF KANSAS_IN THE HANDS OF THE "BORDER RUFFIANS".

▲ *This political cartoon is an attack on Franklin Pierce and other high ranking Democrats of the time. They are being blamed for the violence caused by Border Ruffians in Kansas. This image was drawn by John L. Magee.*

volunteers prepared to defend their town. An estimated two thousand volunteers built fortifications and kept a watchful eye out for their invaders. As the two sides braced for an armed confrontation, Governor Shannon took on the role of the peacemaker.

Governor Shannon had been concerned that the influx of the Border Ruffians would lead to an armed conflict. On December 4, he met with some antislavery leaders who expressed their concerns that the Border Ruffians would invade and destroy their town. Two days later, he visited the campsite of the pro-slavery forces. On December 8, Shannon was able to broker a peace treaty.

Both sides signed a written statement that said the citizens of Lawrence were not to blame for Branson's escape from Sheriff Jones and his posse. The statement also said that the citizens of Lawrence would aid in any legal actions against criminals, but it did not clearly define the term legal action. Furthermore, the antislavery forces maintained that nothing in the statement obligated them to obey any laws passed by the territorial legislature.

Once the agreement was signed, Governor Shannon ordered the military forces encamped outside of Lawrence to disband. He assured the proslavery leaders that he had made "satisfactory agreements" to ensure that the laws would be enforced.

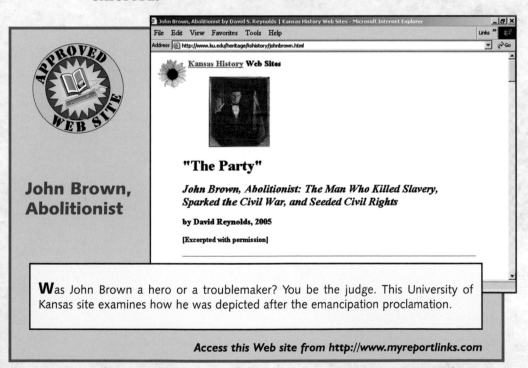

John Brown, Abolitionist

John Brown, Abolitionist by David S. Reynolds | Kansas History Web Sites - Microsoft Internet Explorer

File   Edit   View   Favorites   Tools   Help

Address http://www.ku.edu/heritage/kshistory/johnbrown.html

Kansas History **Web Sites**

"The Party"

John Brown, Abolitionist: The Man Who Killed Slavery, Sparked the Civil War, and Seeded Civil Rights

by David Reynolds, 2005

[Excerpted with permission]

Was John Brown a hero or a troublemaker? You be the judge. This University of Kansas site examines how he was depicted after the emancipation proclamation.

Access this Web site from http://www.myreportlinks.com

No Federal Intervention

At about the same time, the 34th Congress was convening in Washington. In his annual message to Congress, President Pierce only devoted one paragraph to the situation in Kansas. Pierce merely acknowledged that there had been some problems, but he believed that nothing was serious enough to merit the intervention of the federal government.

A Temporary Peace

The peaceable end to a war without bloodshed or battles was viewed differently in the North than it was in the South. Antislavery Northerners saw it as a triumph for freedom. Pro-slavery Southerners regarded it as a triumph of lawlessness and a disgraceful show of appeasement by their side.

The peace would not be a lasting one. Within months, Lawrence would come under siege of the pro-slavery forces. John Brown and his cohorts would retaliate, and the Kansas Territory would become known as Bleeding Kansas.

Chapter 4 ▶

PRO-SLAVERY FORCES TAKE CONTROL

As the rest of the nation rang in the New Year of 1856, Kansas was truly becoming a territory with two governments preparing to fight an undeclared war. On January 15, the Free-Soil Kansans held their own election. They elected Charles Robinson as their governor and elected members of their own legislature. Governor Shannon called on President Pierce to send in federal troops to keep the peace. On January 24, Pierce responded with a special message to Congress. Pierce's message angered and dismayed the free-staters.

Pierce admitted to Congress that there had been "irregularities" in the formation of the territorial government, but he called the recently elected legislature in Topeka "legitimate." He denounced the election held by the free-staters as an act of "rebellion." He threatened to send in federal troops and asked Congress to approve funding for it.

In February, Pierce went even further by putting the federal troops stationed at Fort Leavenworth, Kansas, at Governor Shannon's disposal. That did not deter the free-state

▲ William Seward was a senator from New York who proposed to the Senate that Kansas be admitted as a state under the state constitution Kansans passed banning slavery. He later became a member of President Lincoln's Cabinet.

forces. They met in Topeka to form their own government. On March 4, they petitioned Congress to admit them to the Union.

The Republicans in Congress supported the antislavery government. They were the majority party in the House of Representatives, but the Democrats still controlled the Senate. Senator Douglas was able to delay the process. He introduced a bill that required Kansas to hold a new constitutional convention before it could be admitted to the Union.

Three days after Douglas introduced his bill, the Republicans responded with a bill of their own. Senator William Seward of New York proposed that Kansas be admitted under the constitution passed by the free-staters. Seward's bill passed in the House but was rejected by the Senate.

▶ Attack on Charles Sumner

In May 1856, the congressional debate over Kansas's statehood led to the brutal beating of a Republican senator by a Democratic congressman. Senator Charles Sumner of Massachusetts delivered a two-day speech he had entitled "The Crime Against Kansas." Sumner's speech went well beyond the boundaries of partisan disagreement. The language was scathing and unrestrained. He attacked Senator Douglas by comparing him to a "noisome, squat and nameless animal."[1]

Sumner saved his most scornful remarks for Senator Andrew Butler of South Carolina. Sumner compared Butler's support of slavery to a man who takes on a mistress. Sumner said Butler "has chosen a mistress to whom he has made his vows, and who, though ugly to others, is always lovely to him: though polluted in the sight of the world is chaste in his sight . . . the harlot slavery."[2]

Sumner's speech incensed many people. Among them was South Carolina Congressman Preston Brooks, who was Butler's nephew. Brooks thought that Sumner's speech was a libelous and

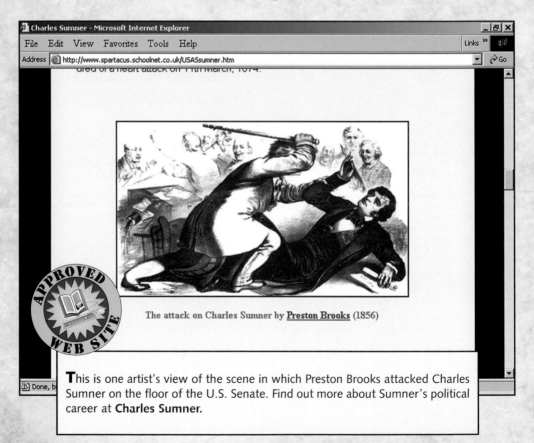

Charles Sumner - Microsoft Internet Explorer

File   Edit   View   Favorites   Tools   Help   Links »

Address http://www.spartacus.schoolnet.co.uk/USASsumner.htm   Go

The attack on Charles Sumner by **Preston Brooks** (1856)

This is one artist's view of the scene in which Preston Brooks attacked Charles Sumner on the floor of the U.S. Senate. Find out more about Sumner's political career at **Charles Sumner.**

uncalled for attack on both his state and his uncle. Brooks decided that the only remedy was to give Senator Sumner a sound beating.

On May 22, 1856, Brooks entered the Senate chamber carrying an eleven-and-a-half ounce cane, a sturdy walking stick. He found Sumner sitting at his desk. Brooks walked up to the senator and calmly said, "I have read your speech twice over, carefully; it is a libel on South Carolina and Mr. Butler who is a relative of mine."[3]

Without waiting for an answer, Brooks began beating Sumner about the head and shoulders with the cane. The beating lasted less than a minute, but it caused severe head injuries. It took Sumner nearly two-and-a-half years to fully recover and resume his duties in the Senate on a full-time basis.

Brooks would later recall, "Every lick went where I intended . . . I . . . gave him about 30 first-rate stripes (blows). I wore my cane out completely . . ."[4]

Reaction to the Attack

Northerners were outraged and appalled by the savage attack. Southerners saw it as a man defending the honor of his family and his state. A House committee would later recommend that Brooks be expelled from Congress, but the motion was not approved by the House. Brooks resigned

▲ Preston Brooks was a member of the U.S. House of Representatives from South Carolina. His attack on Charles Sumner was so vicious that it took Sumner over three years to recover.

his seat, but he was reelected and returned to the House. Fearing further outbreaks of violence, members of Congress began carrying firearms while going about their daily business.

Assassination Attempt

About the time Sumner was making his infamous speech, the uneasy truce between the pro-slavery and antislavery factions in Kansas was unraveling. On April 19, Sheriff Jones and one of his deputies entered Lawrence to make an arrest. They were seeking out a man named S. N. Wood. Wood had helped Jacob Branson escape from Sheriff Jones's custody in November 1854.

They were rebuffed and disarmed by a crowd of antislavery residents. Jones came back the next day with a posse to back him up. Still, he was unable to make the arrest. A crowd gathered and refused to turn over Wood. When the sheriff said he was invoking the "laws of the Kansas Territory," the crowd responded with threats and shouted, "[W]e will never submit."[5]

Sheriff Jones decided that he could no longer tolerate their defiance. Three days later, he returned to Lawrence with some United States troops. With the backing of the troops, Jones was able to make six arrests, but was unable to locate Wood. Jones decided to try again the next day, so he set up camp outside of Lawrence. At around

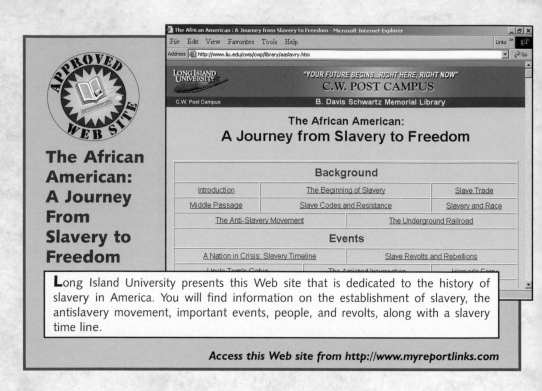

The African American: A Journey From Slavery to Freedom

The African American : A Journey from Slavery to Freedom - Microsoft Internet Explorer

File   Edit   View   Favorites   Tools   Help   Links »

Address http://www.liu.edu/cwis/cwp/library/aaslavry.htm   Go

LONG ISLAND UNIVERSITY   "YOUR FUTURE BEGINS...RIGHT HERE, RIGHT NOW"
                              C.W. POST CAMPUS
C.W. Post Campus   B. Davis Schwartz Memorial Library

The African American:
A Journey from Slavery to Freedom

Background		
Introduction	The Beginning of Slavery	Slave Trade
Middle Passage	Slave Codes and Resistance	Slavery and Race
The Anti-Slavery Movement		The Underground Railroad

Events	
A Nation in Crisis: Slavery Timeline	Slave Revolts and Rebellions
Uncle Tom's Cabin	The Amistad Insurrection	Harper's Ferry

Long Island University presents this Web site that is dedicated to the history of slavery in America. You will find information on the establishment of slavery, the antislavery movement, important events, people, and revolts, along with a slavery time line.

Access this Web site from http://www.myreportlinks.com

ten o'clock at night, he was shot in the back while sitting in his tent.

Jones recovered from the gunshot, but the proslavery faction was determined to retaliate. The newspaper, the *Atchison Squatter Sovereign,* stirred things up by erroneously reporting that Jones had been murdered. They ran a headline:

THE ABOLITIONISTS ARE IN OPEN REBELLION—
SHERIFF JONES MURDERED BY THE TRAITORS.[6]

After the assassination attempt on Sheriff Jones, J. W. Whitfield claimed that witnesses felt that it was not safe for them to come to Lawrence. Most of the witnesses insisted on testifying in places compatible with their political views. Pro-slavery witnesses testified in Lecompton or Leavenworth. Antislavery witnesses testified in Lawrence.

In Lawrence, the antislavery leaders held a public meeting and denounced the attack on Jones. Reeder called it an "outrage," but Robinson hinted that it was the work of a pro-slavery group. Other antislavery leaders labeled it an "isolated act" of an "individual." They hoped that their meeting and public statements would calm things down. However, it did little to ease the escalating tensions.

Legal issues were making the situation more tense. A congressional investigating committee was in Kansas to investigate claims of election fraud. They were also empowered to decide whether Whitfield or Andrew H. Reeder would be seated as the territory's congressional delegate. The committee had chosen the Free State Hotel in Lawrence as its meeting place.

Antislavery Leaders Jailed

On May 5, Samuel D. Lecompte, chief justice of the United States District Court, told a grand jury to indict the leaders of the free-state movement and to close down the newspapers and hotel in Lawrence as public nuisances. The hotel had concerned the pro-slavery forces because it was built like a fortress. The basement walls were two feet thick, and there were also walls that rose two to six feet above the hotel's roof. The rooftop walls had covered portholes that could easily be converted into gun ports for snipers.

Antislavery leaders learned about the indictments ahead of time when a grand juror from Lawrence leaked the news. A subpoena was issued for Reeder. At first, he ignored it; then he asked the congressional committee to protect him since he had been elected as the territory's delegate to Congress. The committee refused to protect him, so Reeder fled Kansas. He stayed in several different safe houses until antislavery sympathizers smuggled him into Kansas City, Missouri.

"Governor" Robinson, the man the free-staters unofficially elected, attempted to quietly flee. He was captured in Lexington, Missouri. There were concerns that he might be assassinated by his captors, but he was treated humanely.

▶ Impending Doom

The prevailing mood in Lawrence was a feeling of impending doom. The Free-Soil leaders had become either fugitives or captives. The proslavery forces had formed patrols that sought out and harassed peaceful travelers and residents. According to one unnamed witness:

> Camps were formed at different points along the highways and on the Kansas River, and peaceful travelers were subject to detention, robbery, and

▲ *Charles Robinson was the man the Free State party supporters chose as governor of Kansas. President Pierce did not agree that Robinson should be governor.*

insult. Men were stopped in the streets and on the open prairie, and bidden to stand and deliver their purses at the peril of their lives. Cattle, provisions, arms, and other property were taken whenever found without consent of the owners. Men were choked from their horses, which were seized by the marauders, and houses were broken open and pillaged of their contents.[7]

In mid-May 1856, a gang of Border Ruffians surrounded the village of Benicia, which was only seven miles away from Lawrence. They rounded up the village residents, who were mainly originally from the North, and herded them into a cabin. The gang leader sternly warned them that the Kansas Territory belonged to the South and that they had no right to be there. He threatened to hang them if they did not leave.

▶ Posse Comes to Town

To carry out the orders of the grand jury, Sheriff Jones led a federal marshal and posse into Lawrence. Several city leaders had petitioned Governor Shannon and U.S. Marshal Israel Donelson to send in federal troops to protect people and property in Lawrence. Shannon's response was to merely acknowledge that a marshal and a posse were nearby. The governor did not acknowledge that a force of pro-slavery Border Ruffians, estimated at five hundred to seven hundred men, was surrounding Lawrence.

The posse had been formed by the sheriff and the federal marshal without the knowledge and consent of the governor. The governor was not in control of the situation, and he was not making any effort to intervene.

The residents of Lawrence realized that resistance was futile. They issued a statement declaring that they would not resist "the execution of the laws, national or territorial."[8]

Sack of Lawrence

On the morning of May 21, 1856, the citizens of Lawrence awakened to see hundreds of Border Ruffians and a battery of four cannons aimed at their city. That same morning, a United States

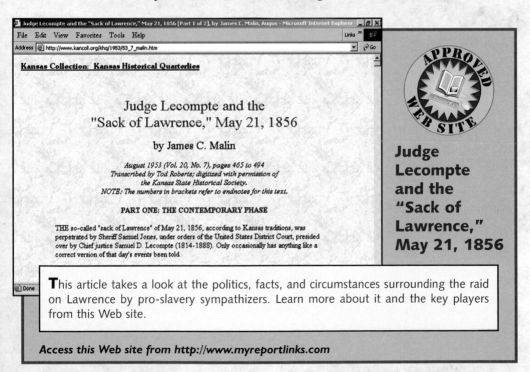

Judge Lecompte and the "Sack of Lawrence," May 21, 1856

This article takes a look at the politics, facts, and circumstances surrounding the raid on Lawrence by pro-slavery sympathizers. Learn more about it and the key players from this Web site.

Access this Web site from http://www.myreportlinks.com

deputy marshal rode into town and quietly made some arrests. The marshal and his men encountered no resistance or apparent hostility.

Around mid-afternoon, Sheriff Jones rode into town and instructed the townspeople to surrender their arms. After disarming them, Jones announced that he would carry out the grand jury's order to raze the Free State Hotel and destroy the newspapers. The hotel manager was given a deadline of five o'clock in the evening for removing furniture, fixtures, and other property from the building.

The Hotel Is Attacked

After clearing the area around the hotel, the posse began firing on the hotel. There was a cannon aimed directly at the structure. Senator Atchison claimed the honor of firing the first shot. Atchison's shot completely missed the hotel and soared over the roof. According to one account, Atchison's aim was off because he had been drinking too much.[9]

About another thirty shots were fired, but the only damage inflicted was some holes in the hotel's sturdy concrete walls. Then, the posse tried to blow up the hotel by igniting two kegs of gunpowder they placed in the basement. The explosion shattered the windows, but failed to bring down the building.

▲ David Rice Atchison was a senator from Missouri who supported the Border Ruffians that wished to make Kansas a slave state.

Finally, the posse resorted to arson. While the hotel was aflame, Sheriff Jones proudly told his posse, "Gentlemen, this is the happiest day of my life. I determined to make the fanatic bow before me in the dust and kiss the territorial laws. I have done it, by God. You are now dismissed."[10]

▶ The Town is Looted

Once they were officially dismissed, the posse of Border Ruffians went on a looting spree. A few officers tried to stop the pillaging by shouting at them to stop. Their shouts were ignored. Homes and businesses were entered, and the posse took anything they wanted.

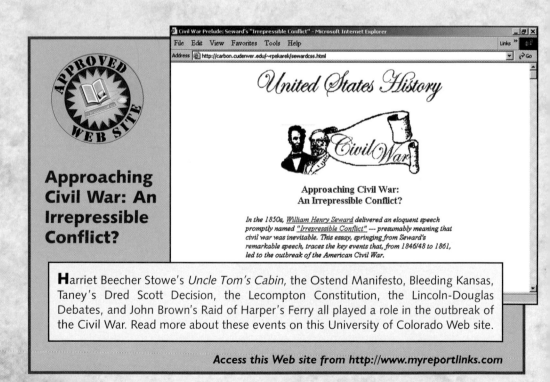

Approaching Civil War: An Irrepressible Conflict?

United States History

Approaching Civil War: An Irrepressible Conflict?

In the 1850s, William Henry Seward delivered an eloquent speech promptly named "Irrepressible Conflict" --- presumably meaning that civil war was inevitable. This essay, springing from Seward's remarkable speech, traces the key events that, from 1846/48 to 1861, led to the outbreak of the American Civil War.

Harriet Beecher Stowe's *Uncle Tom's Cabin*, the Ostend Manifesto, Bleeding Kansas, Taney's Dred Scott Decision, the Lecompton Constitution, the Lincoln-Douglas Debates, and John Brown's Raid of Harper's Ferry all played a role in the outbreak of the Civil War. Read more about these events on this University of Colorado Web site.

Access this Web site from http://www.myreportlinks.com

Along with the looting, there was substantial property damage. Robinson's home was burned. The newspaper presses were vandalized and then dumped in the Kansas River. Books and newspapers were burned in the streets. The Border Ruffians helped themselves to liquor found in the hotel's basement and in homes. Many of the looters were drunk and staggering in the streets.

The looting finally ended shortly after sundown. Only one person was killed in the Sack of Lawrence. The lone victim was a pro-slavery Southerner who was killed by a stone falling from the hotel. The unarmed free staters had offered no resistance.

▶ Heroes or Villains

In the pro-slavery areas of Kansas and in Missouri, the returning Border Ruffians were hailed as conquering heroes. But, for anyone who opposed slavery or had been neutral on the issue, the Sack of Lawrence was an appalling spectacle. People who had considered the antislavery settlers as rebels for defying territorial laws, now admired them for passively refraining from violence.

Not all of the antislavery settlers thought that passive resistance was the best plan. The most notable exception was John Brown and his cohorts. After learning about the Sack of Lawrence, they brutally attacked and murdered five pro-slavery settlers on the night of May 24. Their attack would come to be called the Pottawatomie Massacre. The news of the Sack of Lawrence and the Pottawatomie Massacre forced the country to focus on the violence in the Kansas Territory.

The problems of Bleeding Kansas would greatly influence the 1856 presidential election, end the presidency of Franklin Pierce, and help to make a little known Illinois lawyer named Abraham Lincoln a national political figure.

RATIFYING A CONSTITUTION PROVES DIFFICULT

When the Democrats and Republicans held their national conventions in June 1856, the issue of whether slavery would expand into Kansas was a prominent part of their proceedings. The Republicans assembled in Philadelphia, and they treated the Kansas Territory as a state. The young party allowed antislavery Kansans to send a full slate of voting delegates to its first national convention. To further emphasize their opposition to slavery, the Republicans omitted delegations from the Deep South. However, the border slave states of Delaware, Maryland, Virginia, and Kentucky, as well as the District of Columbia, were allowed to send voting delegations.

▶ John C. Frémont

After only one ballot, the Republicans nominated John C. Frémont of California as their first presidential candidate. Frémont was considered a political novice, although he had served as one of California's first two U.S. Senators in 1850–51. Frémont was better known for his exploits as an

▲ John C. Frémont was the Republican candidate for president in 1856.

explorer and soldier. His pioneering expeditions of the Rocky Mountains, California, Oregon, and other parts of the American West earned him the nickname "The Pathfinder."

Frémont's antislavery views were well known, but his views on other issues were largely unknown. Some of his political opponents made the false claim that Frémont had once owned slaves. The platform adopted by the Republicans in 1856 opposed popular sovereignty—the expansion of slavery into territories—and called for the admission of Kansas as a free state. Their platform also blamed the Pierce administration for the violence and unrest in Kansas.

Democratic Convention

The Democrats held their national convention in Cincinnati with delegations from all thirty-one states. There were three main contenders vying for the party's presidential nomination, including President Franklin Pierce. Initially, Pierce had promised that he would not seek a second term, but he changed his mind. Stephen Douglas was hoping to unseat Pierce, but a third candidate, James Buchanan of Pennsylvania would become the nominee.

Buchanan was a career politician and public servant. He had served in both houses of Congress and as secretary of state from 1845 until 1849.

He had additional diplomatic experience from serving as ambassador to both Russia (1832–33) and Great Britain (1854–56).

All three candidates had defended slavery as being sanctioned by the U.S. Constitution. Buchanan had the advantage of being out of the country during the debate over the Kansas-Nebraska Act and when violence in Kansas became national news. Douglas was tainted by his support of popular sovereignty and the Kansas-Nebraska Act, and people remembered that this had caused the current unrest in Kansas. Pierce was unavoidably associated with Bleeding Kansas because he was unable to stop the violence there.

▶ Candidates Go Back and Forth

The nominee needed to get two thirds of the delegate votes instead of a simple majority. After the first ballot, Buchanan had 135.5 votes, Pierce 122.5, and Douglas 33. After fifteen ballots, Buchanan had 168.5, Douglas 118.5, and Pierce had fallen to only 3.5 votes. Douglas broke the deadlock by withdrawing after the sixteenth ballot. On the seventeenth ballot, Buchanan received all 296 votes.

Since Buchanan was from the free state of Pennsylvania, the party balanced the ticket by giving him a running mate from a slave state. Kentucky congressman John C. Breckinridge was chosen as the candidate for vice president.

▶ Democratic Support for Kansas-Nebraska Act

The party platform adopted by the Democrats endorsed both the Compromise of 1850 and the Kansas-Nebraska Act. The platform praised the Kansas-Nebraska Act as "the only sound and safe solution to the slavery problem."[1] The Democratic platform also opposed any federal interference with slavery. The platform failed to address the issue of whether slavery could be banned from a territory before it was ready for statehood.

Democrats who had hoped that their party would take a stand against the expansion of slavery were sorely disappointed. For them, the

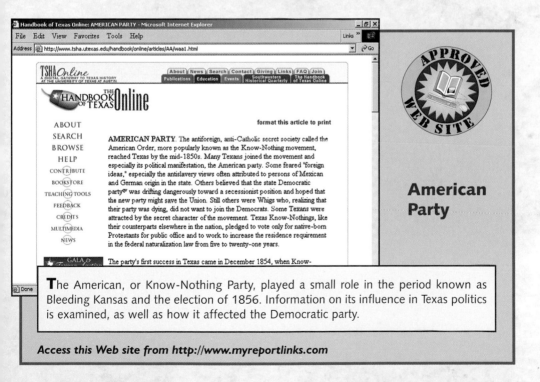

American Party

The American, or Know-Nothing Party, played a small role in the period known as Bleeding Kansas and the election of 1856. Information on its influence in Texas politics is examined, as well as how it affected the Democratic party.

Access this Web site from http://www.myreportlinks.com

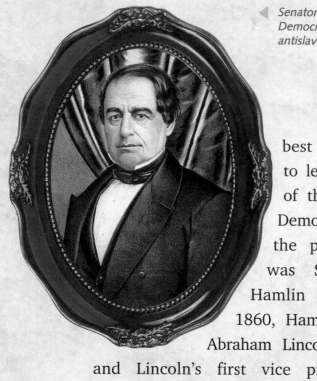

Senator Hannibal Hamlin left the Democratic party because he was antislavery.

best alternative was to leave the party. One of the most prominent Democrats to break with the party over slavery was Senator Hannibal Hamlin of Maine. (In 1860, Hamlin would become Abraham Lincoln's running mate and Lincoln's first vice president.) Hamlin expressed his disgust with the Democrats by saying, "The old Dem. party is now the party of slavery. It has no other issue in fact and this is the standard on which it measures every thing and every man."[2]

A third party, called the American or Know-Nothing party, nominated ex-president Millard Fillmore as their presidential candidate. They opposed any federal interference with slavery and believed that popular sovereignty should decide the issue of slavery in the territories. However, they were best known for their anti-Catholic views. They believed that all public offices should be held only by native-born, non-Catholic Americans. Their slogan said that Americans must rule America.

The Toombs Bill

After being denied renomination, Pierce spent his final months as president vainly trying to solve the problem of Bleeding Kansas. There were pleas from Kansans asking him to send federal troops there to maintain law and order. He responded by telegraphing Kansas authorities. In his telegraphs, Pierce urged them to use the federal troops already there to preserve order and enforce the law.

Pierce threw his support behind a proposal known as the Toombs Bill. The bill proposed that

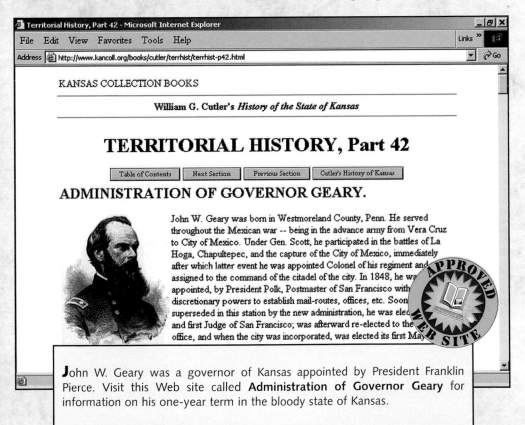

John W. Geary was a governor of Kansas appointed by President Franklin Pierce. Visit this Web site called **Administration of Governor Geary** for information on his one-year term in the bloody state of Kansas.

▲ *John W. Geary was a territorial governor of Kansas, and later became a major general in the Civil War.*

a statewide election would be held in Kansas after a census was taken. Only residents who had lived in Kansas for three months or longer at the time of the census could vote. That would prevent pro-slavery or antislavery forces from flooding into Kansas before the election. The voters would elect delegates to a constitutional convention. The constitution they drafted would determine if slavery would be allowed in Kansas.

The bill passed the Senate, but the House refused to even consider it. A coalition of Whigs, Democrats, and Know-Nothings kept it from coming up for a vote.

In late July 1856, Pierce removed Shannon as governor of Kansas and replaced him with John W. Geary of Pennsylvania. Geary's appointment had a brief, calming effect, but partisan politics hampered efforts to bring a lasting peace.

Congress at Odds With the President

The same forces in the House that doomed the Toombs Bill, made it difficult for Pierce to use federal troops in Kansas. They added an amendment to an army appropriation bill that forbade the president from using federal troops to enforce laws passed by a territorial legislature. The amendment was probably unconstitutional, but it would have taken the courts months or years to decide that.

The amendment did not get approved by the Senate, so soldiers did not get their pay. Congress tried to adjourn without settling the issue. Pierce stopped them by calling for a special session of Congress.

Knowing that federal troops could not interfere in Kansas emboldened both the antislavery and pro-slavery forces. Fear of an all out civil war forced Congress to act. The House passed a bill that paid the soldiers and gave the president unrestricted power to use federal troops to preserve order in Kansas.

The Election of 1856

None of the three presidential candidates campaigned in the manner we see today. At that time, the speech making and handshaking was done by other party members and officeholders. Buchanan made his views known by writing carefully scripted letters to newspapers. Frémont made appearances at political rallies, but he left the making of speeches to other party leaders.

In the November election, Buchanan received 45 percent of the vote. Frémont trailed with 33 percent, and Fillmore received the remaining 22 percent. Buchanan won every slave state except for Maryland. The upstart Republican party won the electoral votes of eleven of the sixteen free

▲ *Millard Fillmore had been the thirteenth president of the United States. He ran for president again in the election of 1856 as the Know-Nothing party candidate.*

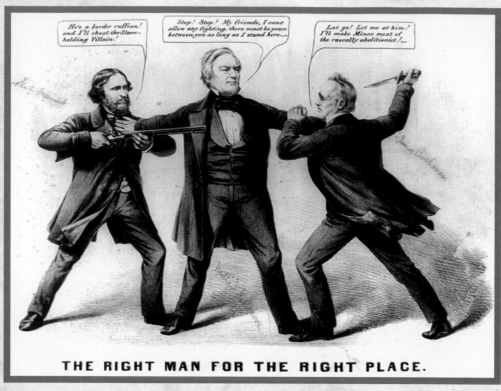

THE RIGHT MAN FOR THE RIGHT PLACE.

▲ This political cartoon supports Millard Fillmore for the election of 1856. He is shown in the middle as the peacekeeper between John Frémont (left) and James Buchanan (right). Of the three, Fillmore received the fewest Votes.

states. The electoral vote totals were Buchanan 174, Frémont 114, and Fillmore 8.

Some Republican leaders hailed the election as a "victorious defeat" for their party. They nominated a candidate who had never held public office and received over 1.3 million of the 4 million votes cast. They also gained five seats in the Senate, but lost sixteen seats in the House.

Between his election and his inauguration, Buchanan picked his Cabinet. His actions showed that loyalty to him was more important than ability or experience. Even though Senator Douglas had made Buchanan's nomination and election possible by stepping aside, Buchanan snubbed him. None of Douglas's prominent supporters received a Cabinet post.

Republicans were also excluded in spite of their growing strength and influence. In a December 1856 letter to a friend, Buchanan made his feelings about abolitionists and Republicans known by writing, "The great object of my administration will be to arrest (stop), if possible, the agitation of the slavery question at the North and to destroy sectional parties."[3]

President Buchanan

On March 4, 1857, James Buchanan was inaugurated as America's fifteenth president. During his lengthy inaugural address, he asserted that Congress had no authority to allow or prohibit slavery in the territories. It could only be decided by the will of the people residing there. In other words, he supported what he saw as the right of slaveholders to settle into new territories with their slaves. He supported the view that slaves were merely property, like cattle or horses.

Four years earlier, Pierce had addressed the slavery issue in his inaugural address by saying, "I believe that involuntary servitude, as it exists in

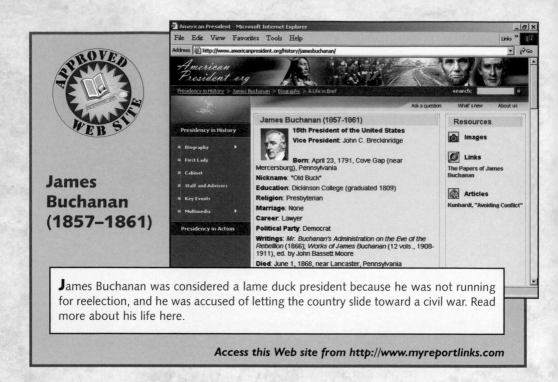

James Buchanan (1857-1861)

15th President of the United States
Vice President: John C. Breckinridge

Born: April 23, 1791, Cove Gap (near Mercersburg), Pennsylvania
Nickname: "Old Buck"
Education: Dickinson College (graduated 1809)
Religion: Presbyterian
Marriage: None
Career: Lawyer
Political Party: Democrat
Writings: *Mr. Buchanan's Administration on the Eve of the Rebellion* (1866); *Works of James Buchanan* (12 vols., 1908-1911), ed. by John Bassett Moore
Died: June 1, 1868, near Lancaster, Pennsylvania

James Buchanan (1857–1861)

James Buchanan was considered a lame duck president because he was not running for reelection, and he was accused of letting the country slide toward a civil war. Read more about his life here.

Access this Web site from http://www.myreportlinks.com

different States of this Confederacy, is recognized by the Constitution. . . . I fervently hope that the question is at rest . . ."[4]

Like Pierce, Buchanan had hoped that the issue would simply go away. Buchanan expressed a similar view, but in his inaugural address the new president took the issue even further by blaming the abolitionists for stirring up the issue.

May we not, then, hope that the long agitation on this subject is approaching its end. . . . Throughout the whole progress of this agitation, which has scarcely known any intermission for more than twenty years, whilst it has been productive of no positive good to any human being it has been the prolific source of great evils to the master, to the slave, and to the whole country.[5]

▶ Dred Scott

Only two days after Buchanan was inaugurated, the U.S. Supreme Court issued a far-reaching landmark decision that greatly pleased the pro-slavery forces. In the case of *Dred Scott v. Sanford,* the court ruled the 1820 Missouri Compromise was unconstitutional and that slaves were property and not people with legal rights.

Dred Scott was a slave who had been taken by his owner from the slave state of Missouri to the free state of Illinois. After being taken back into

The *Dred Scott* Case

Washington University Libraries presents a Web site dedicated to the *Dred Scott* case, along with scans of historical documents. A chronology of events is included, with a link to case files of other freedom suits.

Access this Web site from http://www.myreportlinks.com

Missouri, Scott sued for his freedom by claiming that the time he spent in a free state had made him a free man.

The court ruled that since Scott was a slave, he was not a United States citizen. The court's decision also declared that slaveholders had the right to take their property anywhere they wished. That meant that Congress could not outlaw slavery in any territory. However, a territory could outlaw slavery after it became a state.

▶ The Decision

Buchanan had been well aware of the impending decision. He had been closely following the case and had used the power and prestige of his position as president-elect to influence the decision. When he was inaugurated, he already knew how the Supreme Court was going to rule. He had written a letter to Associate Justice Robert Grier asking him to support a decision making the Missouri Compromise unconstitutional. Buchanan had vainly hoped that a Supreme Court decision would finally and decisively settle the issue of slavery.

The 7–2 decision went far beyond anything Buchanan could have hoped for. Instead of settling the slavery issue, it outraged abolitionists and inflamed passions. The court ruled that all blacks, slave or free, were not and could never be

The **Abolition, Anti-Slavery Movements, and the Rise of the Sectional Controversy** Web page from the Library of Congress provides plenty of information about the Fugitive Slave Law. This photo was taken at a mission for fugitive slaves in Canada.

American citizens. Chief Justice Roger Taney declared that "they [blacks] were not included and not intended to be included, under the word 'citizens' in the Constitution."[6]

▶ Territorial Governor Geary

On the same day Buchanan was inaugurated, John W. Geary resigned as governor of the Kansas Territory. Geary had been the third and last territorial governor to be appointed by Pierce. Geary had managed the difficult task of protecting the rights of antislavery settlers while recognizing the pro-slavery legislature as the legitimate govern-ment. Geary had found that serving as governor was a thankless task, and he was frustrated by the lack of support from the Pierce administration.

Geary had tried and failed to reform the territorial court system. He wanted to see justice served without regard to politics. While Geary was governor, Charles Hays, a known killer of an antislavery settler, was arrested. Judge Lecompte ordered Hays to be released. Geary had him rear-rested, and then a pro-slavery grand jury indicted Hays on a first-degree murder charge. Yet, Lecompte freed Hays on bail. Geary was so out-raged that he asked Pierce to remove Lecompte from office. Pierce failed to support Geary and Lecompte stayed in office.

▶ Robert Walker

Buchanan appointed Robert Walker of Mississippi to succeed Geary as territorial governor. Walker did have some truly impressive credentials. He was a former United States senator, secretary of the treasury, and the son of a U.S. Supreme Court justice. Walker's wife did not want him to take the post, but his sense of duty made him accept it. Walker would often compare his appointment to that of a soldier being ordered into combat.

▲ James Buchanan was the fifteenth president of the United States. It was during his administration that the Southern states began to secede from the Union.

The Question of Slavery in Kansas

Despite all of the violence that had preceded his appointment, Walker believed that the slavery issue could be settled peaceably by a fair and free election. In a letter to his sister, Walker wrote; "The slavery question in Kansas is not so unsolvable. . . . It is reduced to the simple issue, of slave or free state, and must be decided by a full and fair vote of a majority of the people of Kansas. The same question has thus been decided in every other state, and why not in Kansas?"[7]

After dispatching Walker to Kansas, Buchanan publicly supported a statewide election deciding if Kansas would become a free state or a slave state. In his annual message to Congress in December 1857, he said he was neutral on the slavery issue.

> A constitution shall be submitted to the people of the Territory, [and] they must be protected in their right of voting for or against that instrument and the fair expression of the popular will must not be interrupted by fraud and violence . . . it [is] far from my intention to interfere with the decision of the people of Kansas, either for or against slavery.[8]

While Buchanan was proclaiming his neutrality, he was keeping a watchful eye on statewide political conventions in Mississippi and Georgia.

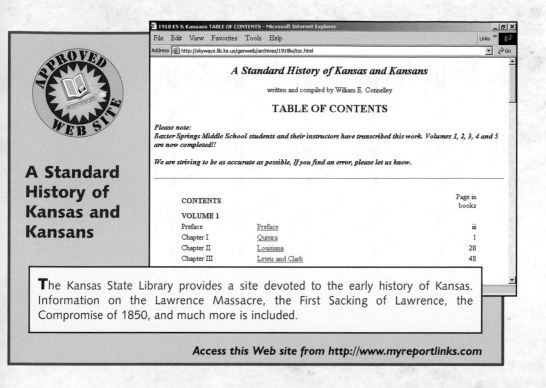

A Standard History of Kansas and Kansans

The Kansas State Library provides a site devoted to the early history of Kansas. Information on the Lawrence Massacre, the First Sacking of Lawrence, the Compromise of 1850, and much more is included.

Access this Web site from http://www.myreportlinks.com

Both states were threatening to secede from the union if Kansas were admitted as a free state.

In June 1857, delegates were elected to write a constitution. Most of the antislavery supporters refused to vote. An estimated seven thousand registered voters stayed away, and only about 10 percent of the eligible voters cast ballots. As a result, about 1,800 pro-slavery voters were able to elect sixty pro-slavery delegates.

The constitutional convention met for only five days in September 1857. They adjourned without deciding when the constitution would be submitted to a popular vote. They knew that if they put the constitution to a popular vote it would never pass into law. They would meet again after a statewide election was held to elect a territorial legislature.

Fraud in Johnson County

The election of representatives to a territorial legislature was held in the first week of October 1857. It was a peaceful election, but once again there was compelling evidence of massive voter fraud. The most blatant case occurred in the Oxford precinct of Johnson County.

The Oxford precinct was located just across from the Missouri state line. There were no reported sightings of bands of Border Ruffians coming in from Missouri, but the number of votes cast greatly exceeded the number of registered voters. Reportedly, 1,628 votes were cast in the Oxford precinct. Those votes helped to elect eight pro-slavery candidates to the legislature. Their election ensured that the pro-slavery forces would have a majority in the new legislature.

Members of the antislavery Free State party decided the investigate the election. They sent a delegation to Johnson County to interview the local election judges. When they arrived, all the judges had left the area and could not be found. The free-staters then asked Governor Walker to investigate.

Walker and Frederick P. Stanton, the territorial secretary of state, made a trip to Johnson County. They were also unable to locate any of the election judges. However, they did find a remarkable document that listed the local voters. The list contained 1,601 names in alphabetical order, and all were written in the same handwriting. When the names were read aloud, witnesses recognized the names of former neighbors in Cincinnati, Ohio. It was determined that the voting list had been copied from a Cincinnati city directory.

Fraud in McGee County

A similar fraud occurred in McGee County. Countywide election returns numbered over one thousand votes, but local residents said there were only about fifty voters in the area. The McGee totals were written in the same handwriting as the voting list from the Oxford precinct.

Governor Walker issued proclamations disallowing the fraudulent votes cast in Johnson and McGee counties. His actions gave the members of the antislavery Free State party a majority in the newly elected legislature.

President Buchanan did not make any public statement about the election fraud, but he was embarrassed by it. He did express gratitude that the election went off peacefully, but Walker felt the president should have endorsed his proclamations.

Shortly after the controversial election, Walker asked Buchanan to grant him a leave of absence during November 1857. Buchanan granted the leave under one condition—Walker would have to stay in Kansas until the constitutional convention was concluded. Walker reluctantly accepted the president's terms.

▷ Lecompton Constitution

Kansas still had a divided government. The newly elected legislature would be controlled by the anti-slavery forces, but the constitutional convention would be controlled by the pro-slavery forces. The delegation that met in Lecompton to write the

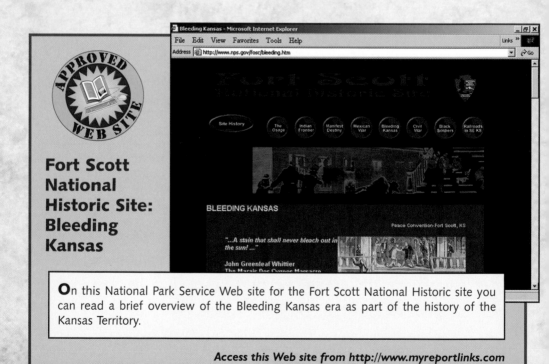

Fort Scott National Historic Site: Bleeding Kansas

On this National Park Service Web site for the Fort Scott National Historic site you can read a brief overview of the Bleeding Kansas era as part of the history of the Kansas Territory.

Access this Web site from http://www.myreportlinks.com

constitution was not a representative sampling of the territory's population.

The antislavery residents had boycotted the election of delegates, so only a small percentage of adult males had elected the delegates. Fifteen Kansas counties were unrepresented. According to the *New York Tribune,* members of the Free State party were totally unrepresented and not a single delegate identified himself as being anti-slavery. It was estimated that about six delegates were slaveholders.

A Fiasco

Along with not being representative of the people, the convention was marked by a lack of common decency. A *New York Tribune* correspondent reported that some delegates were regularly drunk and disorderly throughout the proceedings.

The constitutional convention began on October 19, 1857, and adjourned in early November 1857. Led by chairman John Calhoun, the convention produced a twenty-five-article constitution. The most significant article was Article 7, which favored slavery in the territory.

Article 7 legalized slavery by saying that slaves were property, and it also gave new settlers entering the territory the right to bring their slaves into the territory. At that time, there were around two hundred slaves living in Kansas.

Another Vote

The delegates avoided voting to ratify the new constitution. Their plan was to submit the constitution to Buchanan to submit to Congress. However, Buchanan pledged that the constitution would be submitted to Kansans for ratification in a statewide election. He pressured the delegates to submit the constitution for a statewide vote. A compromise was worked out. Instead of voting on the entire constitution, Kansans would choose between a constitution "with slavery" or "with no slavery." Voting for "with no slavery" merely meant that new settlers could not bring in their slaves. The two hundred or so slaves already in Kansas would not and could not be set free. Nor could the constitution be amended to set them free.

Walker felt that Buchanan had betrayed him. The president had personally assured the governor that the entire constitution would be put to a vote. Walker left Kansas to meet with Buchanan. They had a lengthy personal meeting, but Walker could not persuade the president to change his mind. Buchanan stood firm in supporting both the Lecompton Constitution and the *Dred Scott* decision.

Boycott

On December 21, 1857, Kansans approved the "with slavery" option by a vote of 6,143 to 569.

▲ President Buchanan was a firm supporter of the Dred Scott decision. This is one of the things that may have cost him the election of 1860. This is a sketch of Dred Scott.

Members of the Free State party and other antislavery advocates boycotted the election. Intimidation along with concerns about fraud and violence kept them from voting. The antislavery voters held a separate election in January 1858. In their election, they put the entire constitution to a vote. They rejected the Lecompton Constitution by a vote of 10,266 to 162.

The Buchanan presidency had reached a critical point. He either had to continue to support the Lecompton Constitution or seek a compromise solution to bring peace to the troubled territory.

THE FREE STATE OF KANSAS

The overwhelming rejection of the Lecompton Constitution by the antislavery forces gave Buchanan a chance to change his mind. Such a change would have infuriated Southerners and pro-slavery Kansans, but Buchanan could have said that he was supporting the will of the people. He could have claimed that popular sovereignty had determined that Kansans did not want slavery. Yet, Buchanan continued to push for the ratification of a rejected constitution.

Governor Walker resigned because of President Buchanan's strong support of the Lecompton Constitution. His replacement, James W. Denver, wrote Buchanan after the January election and urged him to reject the Lecompton Constitution and convene a new constitutional convention. Denver warned the president that there would be more violence in Kansas if he supported the controversial new constitution.

Buchanan ignored both Denver's pleas and the election results. Perhaps he was afraid of upsetting the pro-slavery voters who had helped him

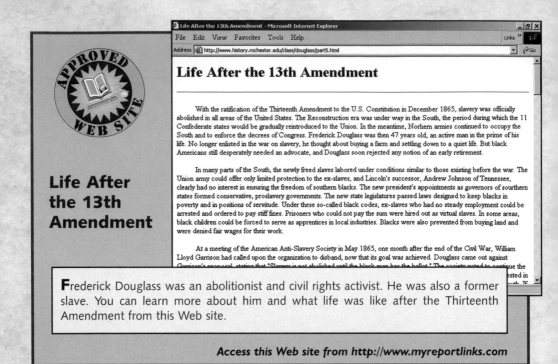

Life After the 13th Amendment

Life After the 13th Amendment

With the ratification of the Thirteenth Amendment to the U.S. Constitution in December 1865, slavery was officially abolished in all areas of the United States. The Reconstruction era was under way in the South, the period during which the 11 Confederate states would be gradually reintroduced to the Union. In the meantime, Norhern armies continued to occupy the South and to enforce the decrees of Congress. Frederick Douglass was then 47 years old, an active man in the prime of his life. No longer enlisted in the war on slavery, he thought about buying a farm and settling down to a quiet life. But black Americans still desperately needed an advocate, and Douglass soon rejected any notion of an early retirement.

In many parts of the South, the newly freed slaves labored under conditions similar to those existing before the war. The Union army could offer only limited protection to the ex-slaves, and Lincoln's successor, Andrew Johnson of Tennessee, clearly had no interest in ensuring the freedom of southern blacks. The new president's appointments as governors of sourthern states formed conservative, proslavery governments. The new state legislatures passed laws designed to keep blacks in poverty and in positions of servitude. Under these so-called black codes, ex-slaves who had no steady employment could be arrested and ordered to pay stiff fines. Prisoners who could not pay the sum were hired out as virtual slaves. In some areas, black children could be forced to serve as apprentices in local industries. Blacks were also prevented from buying land and were denied fair wages for their work.

At a meeting of the American Anti-Slavery Society in May 1865, one month after the end of the Civil War, William Lloyd Garrison had called upon the organization to disband, now that its goal was achieved. Douglass came out against Garrison's proposal, stating that "Slavery is not abolished until the black man has the ballot." The society voted to continue the

Frederick Douglass was an abolitionist and civil rights activist. He was also a former slave. You can learn more about him and what life was like after the Thirteenth Amendment from this Web site.

Access this Web site from http://www.myreportlinks.com

become president. He seemed to be unaware of the depth of feeling slavery was causing. His own party was becoming badly divided over the issue. Senator Stephen Douglas was much more aware of the growing antislavery sentiment. He refused to go along with Buchanan in supporting the Lecompton Constitution. Buchanan then accused him of being disloyal.

▶ Admittance as a Slave State?

On February 2, 1858, Buchanan reaffirmed his support of the Lecompton Constitution in a speech to Congress. He called the antislavery forces in Kansas "mercenaries of abolitionism" and accused them of creating a "revolutionary government."[1] Then he denied that he had ever promised to submit the entire constitution to a statewide vote, only Article 7. Buchanan claimed that when Kansas became a state, it could change any pro-slavery laws. That was a false claim. The Lecompton Constitution came with a provision that it could not be changed for seven years.

Buchanan then asked Congress to admit Kansas to the Union as a slave state under the Lecompton Constitution. He argued that Kansas "at this moment is as much of a slave State as Georgia or South Carolina."[2] Buchanan believed that Kansas entering the Union as a slave state would weaken the Republican party. He had also believed that the *Dred Scott* decision would quiet the abolitionists and end the slavery controversy. He was wrong both times. His insistence on Kansas being a slave state was actually hurting his party and driving thousands of antislavery Democrats into the Republican party.

Douglas Switches Sides

Douglas had a much clearer view of the situation. He saw how Buchanan's support of the Lecompton Constitution was dividing the Democrats and threatening the survival of the Union. Douglas would be up for reelection in 1858 against a formidable Republican challenger named Abraham Lincoln.

▲ *Stephen Douglas felt that the Lecompton Constitution needed to be defeated if the Democrats were to remain in control of the U.S. Congress.*

To Douglas, his political career and the survival of the Democratic party depended on defeating the Lecompton Constitution. In Senate speeches on February 3 and 4, 1858, Douglas condemned the Lecompton Constitution as a violation of popular sovereignty. He questioned whether pro-slavery sentiments really reflected the will of most Kansans.

In March 1858, the Senate voted 33 to 25 to admit Kansas as a slave state under the Lecompton Constitution. The vote was not surprising since the Democrats held thirty-six of the sixty-four senate seats and two thirds of the Democratic senators were from slaveholding states.

Debate in the House of Representatives

To try and get the statehood bill passed in the House, Buchanan used all the political powers and favors at his command. Cabinet members lobbied congressmen and offered inducements that bordered on outright bribery. Government shipbuilding and mail route contracts were offered to congressmen for supporting the president. There were also reports of cash bribes being offered to uncommitted congressmen.

The debate in the House over Kansas statehood got so heated that an all-out brawl erupted. Pennsylvania Republican Galusha Grow and South Carolina Democrat Lawrence Keitt started exchanging insults. Soon, they were wrestling around on the floor of the house. Somewhere between thirty to fifty congressmen joined in the fracas. The fighting ended after one congressman's wig was yanked off his head. The lawmakers quit fighting and started laughing.

When the fighting and debating was finished, the House passed an amended statehood bill. Buchanan had threatened to veto the bill, but it

passed by a vote of 120 to 112. The House version called for the Lecompton Constitution to be resubmitted for a statewide vote before Kansas could be admitted to the Union.

The English Bill

At this point, Buchanan could have worked to convene a new constitutional convention in

The situation in Bleeding Kansas was one of the things that led to the Civil War. Attacks from Missouri into Kansas continued during the war. This engraving is called "Martial Law" by John Sartain.

Kansas with both the pro-slavery and antislavery factions represented. Instead, he tried another compromise solution. He threw his support behind a proposal called the English Bill. The bill would give Kansas a grant of 4 million acres of land held by the federal government if its citizens voted for the Lecompton Constitution. If Kansas rejected the Lecompton Constitution, then it could not join the union until the territorial population reached ninety-three thousand.

In May 1858, the English Bill passed both houses of Congress, but three months later, Kansans rejected the land grant offer and the Lecompton Constitution by a vote of 11,812 to 1,926. Once again, statehood was delayed, and the debate over the right of Kansans to allow or exclude slavery in the territory remained unsettled.

▶ Marais des Cygnes Massacre

While Congress was debating the English Bill, another appalling atrocity in the Kansas Territory was making national news. On May 19, 1858, a band of Border Ruffians murdered eleven Kansas men and wounded five others in an incident known as the Marais des Cygnes Massacre.

The victims had been captured and summarily executed by the Border Ruffians. It is unknown if the shootings were planned or the result of anger and panic by the Border Ruffians. Whatever the cause, the killings increased public sympathy for the antislavery residents of the territory.

Buchanan's stubborn insistence in supporting the Lecompton Constitution and trying to impose slavery on Kansas doomed the Democrats to big losses in the 1858 midterm congressional elections. The Republicans gained six seats in the Senate and twenty-two in the House, giving it control over the House of Representatives. The Democrats remained the majority party in the Senate. In Buchanan's native state of Pennsylvania, the Democratic vote fell by 20 percent from the 1856 totals.

▶ Douglas Versus Lincoln

The most noteworthy congressional election in 1858 was the senatorial race in Illinois. Buchanan's foe, Senator Douglas, was running for reelection against the Republican nominee, Abraham Lincoln.

In June 1858, Lincoln made an acceptance speech at Illinois's Republican State Convention. Using language from the Bible, Lincoln predicted that slavery would eventually destroy the Union in its present form by saying, "A house divided against itself cannot stand." Then, he elaborated on the phrase by adding, "I believe that this government cannot endure, permanently half slave and half free. I do not expect the Union to be dissolved—I

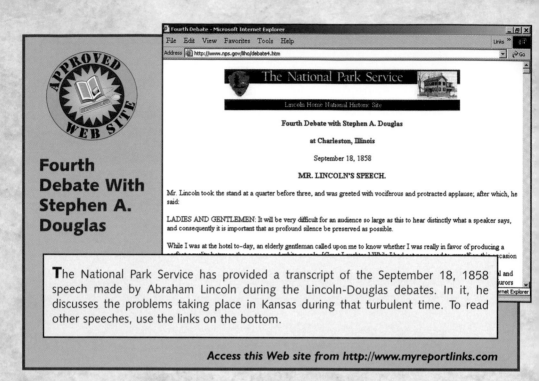

Access this Web site from http://www.myreportlinks.com

do not expect the house to fall—but I do expect that it will cease to be divided. It will become all of one thing, or all the other."[3]

After being nominated, Lincoln challenged Douglas to a series of debates. Douglas accepted the challenge. From August to October 1858, they traveled through Illinois and engaged in a series of seven debates that attracted national attention.

Lincoln argued against the extension of slavery by popular sovereignty or any other means. In his view, slavery was morally wrong and should not be allowed to expand to new parts of the country. Douglas did not view slavery as a moral issue. He continued to argue that the citizens of a state could and should decide if they wanted to allow slavery to exist there. Douglas also asserted that the Union was a government that only allowed free blacks and slaves whatever privileges the white ruling class decided to extend to them. He accused Lincoln of being an abolitionist who believed in social equality between blacks and whites.

At that time, United States senators were elected by state legislatures instead of a direct popular vote. Since the Democrats controlled the state legislature, Douglas was reelected by a vote of 54 to 46. Despite the defeat, Lincoln's speeches and debates with Douglas earned him widespread support from the public.

The Election of 1860

Only two years after defeating Lincoln, Stephen Douglas would be running against him again. This time it was for a higher office—the presidency of the United States. Even before his inauguration, Buchanan had decided to serve only one term. Slavery had so badly divided the Democratic party that many of the Southern delegates walked out of the national convention that nominated Douglas.

The Southern Democrats proceeded to hold a separate convention. They chose Buchanan's vice president, John C. Breckinridge of Kentucky, as their nominee. Breckinridge was endorsed by

▲ Abraham Lincoln's popularity grew nationwide after his debates with Stephen Douglas. He used his new fame to win the election of 1860 and become the nation's sixteenth president.

Buchanan and former presidents, Franklin Pierce and John Tyler.

Old-time Whigs who did not feel comfortable with the Republicans, formed their own party. It was called the Constitutional Union party. They chose John Bell, a former congressman, senator, and Cabinet member from Tennessee, as their nominee.

Since there were four candidates, Lincoln, the Republican nominee, won with only 40 percent of the popular vote. Lincoln did have a solid majority of the electoral vote with 180 talleys to 72 for Breckinridge, 39 for Bell, and only 12 for Douglas.

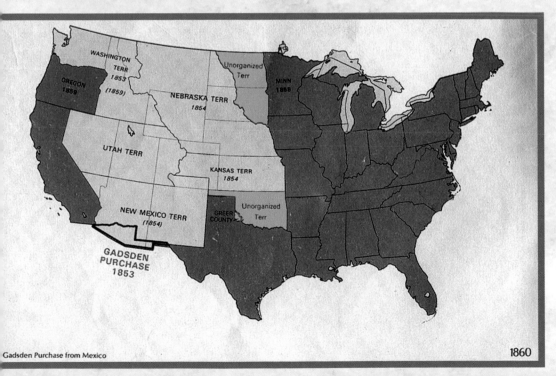

Gadsden Purchase from Mexico

1860

▲ This map shows the borders of the United States as of 1860.

John C. Breckinridge served as vice president under James Buchanan. He ran for president in 1860, but lost.

Secession of the Southern States

After the 1858 midterm elections and the rejection by Kansans of the Lecompton Constitution, Buchanan had turned his attention away from Kansas. He had more pressing issues. Southern states were threatening to secede from the Union. Before Buchanan left office on March 4, 1861, eleven states—South Carolina, Alabama, Florida, Georgia, Louisiana, Mississippi, North Carolina, Arkansas, Tennessee, Virginia, and Texas—withdrew from the Union to form the Confederate States of America. When Lincoln succeeded Buchanan as president in March 1861, the nation was only weeks away from the Civil War.

Kansas Becomes a State

Ironically, one of the last acts of the Buchanan administration was the admission of Kansas to the Union as a free state. On January 29, 1861, the territory that had been labeled Bleeding Kansas became America's thirty-fourth state. After overwhelmingly rejecting the Lecompton Constitution, Kansans elected delegates for another constitutional convention. They adopted and ratified an antislavery constitution, which was sent on to Congress.

In spite of bitter opposition from Southern congressmen and senators, the antislavery constitution was approved by the House in April 1860

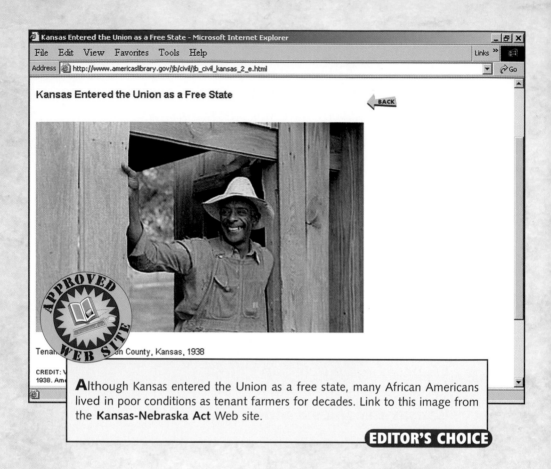

Kansas Entered the Union as a Free State — Microsoft Internet Explorer

File   Edit   View   Favorites   Tools   Help   Links »

Address http://www.americaslibrary.gov/jb/civil/jb_civil_kansas_2_e.html   Go

Kansas Entered the Union as a Free State   BACK

Tenan... ...n County, Kansas, 1938

CREDIT: ...
1938. Am...

Although Kansas entered the Union as a free state, many African Americans lived in poor conditions as tenant farmers for decades. Link to this image from the **Kansas-Nebraska Act** Web site.

EDITOR'S CHOICE

and by the Senate in January 1861. By the time it reached the Senate, the slave states had already seceded from the Union.

▶ The Aftermath of Bleeding Kansas

Historians generally agree that the most lasting effects of Bleeding Kansas were the death of popular sovereignty, the birth of the Republican party, the splitting of the Democratic party, and the foreshadowing of the Civil War. Although the violence and bloodshed of Bleeding Kansas was well reported, it was not extensive. Historians estimate that between fifty and two hundred people were killed in incidents between pro-slavery and anti-slavery supporters in Kansas from 1853 to 1861.

Although they were called battles, the battles of Black Jack, Franklin, Fort Saunders, Hickory Point, and Slough Creek, were mere skirmishes with light casualties. The most notable of the so-called battles was the Battle at Osawatomie. The death toll was only five, but it is remembered because John Brown's son, Frederick, was one of the five. Brown, himself, remained a militant abolitionist. He was eventually hanged to death for his part in the raid on Harpers Ferry, Virginia, which took place in 1859.

The Thirteenth Amendment: The Abolition of Slavery

The University of Missouri-Kansas City School of Law takes a look at the history behind the Thirteenth Amendment, some important constitutional cases, and provisions in the original with regards to slavery.

Access this Web site from http://www.myreportlinks.com

This poster shows the artist's depiction of the trial and execution of abolitionist John Brown.

▶ Who Takes the Blame?

Perhaps a stronger president could have averted some of the violence. Franklin Pierce and James Buchanan have been routinely rated by historians as below average presidents. Both of them are regarded as Northern politicians with Southern sympathies. The presidents viewed slavery as a legal issue and not a moral one. They both considered slaves to be property and not people. Their inability to stop the violence in Kansas led to them becoming one-term presidents.

Lincoln's "house divided" prediction came true. The Union became all of one thing when slavery was abolished with the ratification of the Thirteenth Amendment to the U.S. Constitution in 1865. That was probably the most positive thing to come out of Bleeding Kansas.

Report Links

The Internet sites described below can be accessed at http://www.myreportlinks.com

▶ **Kansas-Nebraska Act**
Editor's Choice A collection of primary documents in American History.

▶ **John Brown's Holy War**
Editor's Choice PBS presents this Web site on the abolitionist John Brown.

▶ **Bleeding Kansas: A Narrative Guide to the Sources**
Editor's Choice This is the story behind the Bleeding of Kansas.

▶ **Territorial Kansas**
Editor's Choice Explore the turbulent times of the Bleeding Kansas days on this site.

▶ **Africans in America**
Editor's Choice This is a comprehensive overview of slavery.

▶ **Topics in Kansas History: Settlement (1830–1890)**
Editor's Choice The Kansas State Historical Society presents a site on the settlement of Kansas.

▶ **Abolition, Anti-Slavery Movements, and the Rise of the Sectional Controversy**
The Library of Congress examines slavery.

▶ **Abraham Lincoln**
A timeline of Lincoln's life is presented on this site.

▶ **Administration of Governor Geary**
This is a comprehensive article on John W. Geary.

▶ **The African American: A Journey From Slavery to Freedom**
Site devoted to understanding the heritage of slavery.

▶ **American Party**
An online resource with an essay on the American party.

▶ **Approaching Civil War: An Irrepressible Conflict?**
This essay discusses the series of events that led to the outbreak of the Civil War.

▶ **Charles Sumner**
An biography of Charles Sumner, who was a prominent abolitionist.

▶ **The *Dred Scott* Case**
Primary documents involved in the *Dred Scott* case can be viewed on this site.

▶ **Eye on John Brown**
Read a modern viewpoint on John Brown in this essay.

Report Links

The Internet sites described below can be accessed at
http://www.myreportlinks.com

▶**Fort Scott National Historic Site: Bleeding Kansas**
Learn more about the turbulent history of the Kansas territory.

▶**Fourth Debate with Stephen A. Douglas**
Read Lincoln's speech in answer to Stephen A. Douglas.

▶**Franklin Pierce**
Read a short biography of President Franklin Pierce on this site.

▶**Harriet Beecher Stowe Center**
This Web site is dedicated to Harriet Beecher Stowe.

▶**Historic Lecompton—Birthplace of the Civil War**
A site dedicated to the history of Lecompton.

▶**James Buchanan (1857–1861)**
This site has a brief biography of President James Buchanan.

▶**John Brown, Abolitionist**
This is an excerpt from a book on slavery.

▶**Judge Lecompte and the "Sack of Lawrence," May 21, 1856**
The Kansas Historical Quarterly presents this essay on the sacking of Lawrence in 1856.

▶**The Kansas-Nebraska Act and the Rise of the Republican Party, 1854-1856**
This is a brief essay on the Kansas-Nebraska Act and Abraham Lincoln.

▶**Life After the 13th Amendment**
What happened when slavery was abolished in the United States?

▶**Missouri Waltz**
This is an interesting article that discusses the push for slavery in Kansas.

▶**Sectional Conflict During the 1850s**
A brief article on how expansionism led to the Civil War.

▶**The "Show Me" State**
An article that looks at Missouri's and the spread of slavery.

▶**A Standard History of Kansas and Kansans**
This is a comprehensive overview of Kansas history.

▶**The Thirteenth Amendment: The Abolition of Slavery**
This site explores constitutional conflicts.

abolitionists—Those aiming to prohibit slavery in the United States.

bidden—To have requested or called upon someone to do a deed.

Blue Lodges—A society of people who recruited pro-slavery settlers to move to the Kansas Territory.

Border Ruffians—People living on the western border of Missouri that bordered the Kansas Territory. They used illegal voting and violence in an effort to try to ensure that Kansas would become a state that allowed slavery.

broadsword—A big sword of considerable weight that was more useful for cutting than for stabbing.

cohorts—Colleagues or companions.

Constitutional Union party—A political group that nominated John Bell in the election of 1860. The members were in favor of maintaining the status quo and continuing the institution of slavery.

Free-Soil—A political party that aimed to keep slavery out of the territories and slave states out of the Union.

free-staters—People who lived in, or supported living in, a state that was free of slavery.

Know-Nothing party—Also known as the American party, it was a secret political organization that aimed to keep immigrants and Catholics out of politics.

libelous—Having written statements that are negative about a person and are often false and damaging to his or her character.

militia—A group of citizens that has organized themselves for military service, or a group of armed citizens that are only called upon in an emergency.

New England Emigrant Aid Company—A company backed by abolitionists that encouraged antislavery settlers to move to the Kansas Territory.

open rebellion—A situation in which anarchy has replaced law and order and citizens are acting in defiance of the government.

partisan—An extreme allegiance to a political party in which a person will follow what the party says to do whether that person thinks the decision is right or wrong.

popular sovereignty—The idea that the people living in territories should vote to determine whether the territory should be a free state or a slave state.

precinct—A division of an area used for the purpose of counting votes in an election.

rebuffed—Rejected.

sanctioned—Officially approved.

Self-Defensives—A society of people who recruited pro-slavery supporters to settle in the Kansas Territory.

territorial legislature—The legislature of a territory of the United States before the territory became a state.

Whig—A supporter of a political party in the United States that was formed in 1834 and supported the financial interests of merchants and business people.

Chapter 1. John Brown and the Pottawatomie Massacre

1. Ken Chowder, "The Father of American Terrorism," *American Heritage,* February/March 2000, p. 82.

2. Peter M. Chaitin, et al, *Story of the Great American West* (Pleasantville, N.Y.: Reader's Digest Association, Inc., 1977), p. 213.

3. Jules Abels, *Man of Fire: John Brown and the Cause of Liberty* (New York: The Macmillan Company, 1971), p. 41.

4. PBS Online, "Pottawatomie Massacre" *People and Events,* 1999, <www.pbs.org./wgbh/amex/brown /peopleevents/pande07.html> (February 22, 2006).

5. Abels, p. 41.

6. Stephen Oates, *To Purge This Land With Blood: A Biography of John Brown* (New York: HarperCollins, 1970), p. 142.

Chapter 2. Free States Versus Slave States

1. T. Harry Williams, *Selected Writings and Speeches of Abraham Lincoln* (New York: Hendricks House, Inc., 1980), p. 42.

2. Mary Beth Norton, et al, *A People & A Nation: A History of the United States: Volume 1: To 1877* (Boston, Houghton Mifflin Company, 1990), p. 381.

3. Ibid, p. 382.

4. Williams, p. 34.

Chapter 3. Tensions Begin to Rise

1. John Gunther, *Inside U.S.A.* (New York: Harper and Brothers, 1947), p. 259.

2. Nicole Etcheson, *Bleeding Kansas Contested Liberty in the Civil War Era* (Lawrence: University Press of Kansas, 2004), p. 32.

3. Ibid. p. 55.

4. Thomas Goodrich, *War to the Knife Bleeding Kansas 1854–1861* (Mechanicsburg, Pa.: Stackpole Books, 1998), p. 57.

5. Etcheson, p. 82.

6. Ibid.

Chapter 4. Pro-Slavery Forces Take Control

1. Nicole Etcheson, *Bleeding Kansas Contested Liberty in the Civil War Era* (Lawrence: University Press of Kansas, 2004), p. 99.

2. Jeff C. Young, *The Fathers of American Presidents* (Jefferson, N.C.: McFarland & Company Publishers, 1997), p. 110.

3. Thomas Goodrich, *War To The Knife Bleeding Kansas 1854–1861* (Mechanicsburg, Pa.: Stackpole Books, 1998), p. 120.

4. Ibid.

5. Etcheson, p. 101.

6. Goodrich, p. 110.

7. Ibid., p. 112.

8. Ibid., p. 104.

9. Michael Schnebly, "The Kansas-Nebraska Bill of 1854: Border Wars Begin," *Bleeding Kansas—Part One,* 2003, <http://www.hahmgs.org /coma2003.html> (February 5, 2006).

10. Goodrich, p. 117.

Chapter 5. Ratifying a Constitution Proves Difficult

1. Arthur M. Schlesinger, Jr., general editor, *The Almanac of American History* (New York: Barnes & Noble Books, 1993), p. 269.

2. Larry Gara, *The Presidency of Franklin Pierce* (Lawrence: University Press of Kansas. 1991), p. 168.

3. Jean H. Baker, *James Buchanan* (New York: Times Books, 2004), p. 80.

4. William A. Degregorio, *The Complete Book of U.S. Presidents* (New York: Barricade Books, 1993), p. 203.

5. Ibid., pp. 217–218.

6. Kenneth M. Stampp, *America in 1857: A Nation on the Brink* (New York: Oxford University Press, 1990), p. 94.

7. Nicole Etcheson, *Bleeding Kansas Contested Liberty in the Civil War Era* (Lawrence: University Press of Kansas, 2004), p. 144.

8. Baker, p. 97.

Chapter 6. The Free State of Kansas

1. Jean H. Baker, *James Buchanan* (New York: Times Books, 2004), p. 102.

2. Elbert B. Smith, *The Presidency of James Buchanan* (Lawrence: University Press of Kansas, 1975), p. 42.

3. Wilson Sullivan, "Abraham Lincoln," *The American Heritage Book of the Presidents and Famous Americans, vol. 5* (New York: Dell Publishing, 1967), p. 408.

Alter, Judy. *Abraham Lincoln.* Berkeley Heights, N.J.: MyReportLinks.com Books, 2002.

Barr, Gary E. *Slavery in the United States.* Chicago: Heinemann Library, 2004.

Becker, Helaine. *John Brown.* Woodridge, Conn.: Blackbirch Press, 2001.

Bjorklund, Ruth. *Kansas.* New York: Benchmark Books, 2000.

Brackett, Virginia. *John Brown: Abolitionist.* Philadelphia: Chelsea House Publishers, 2001.

Doherty, Kieran. *Ranchers, Homesteaders, and Traders: Frontiersmen of the South Central States.* Minneapolis, Minn.: Oliver Press, 2001.

Gunderson, Cory. *The Dred Scott Decision.* Edina, Minn.: Abdo Publishers, 2004.

McArthur, Deborah. *The Kansas-Nebraska Act and "Bleeding Kansas" in American History.* Berkeley Heights, N.J.: Enslow Publishers, Inc., 2003.

Porterfield, Jason. *The Lincoln-Douglas Senatorial Debates of 1858: A Primary Source Investigation.* New York: Rosen Central Primary Sources, 2005.

Zeinert, Karen. *Tragic Prelude: Bleeding Kansas.* North Haven, Conn.: Linnet Books, 2001.